Short Stories by Edogawa Ranpo

Level 5

Translated by
Tom Christian and Morgan Giles

IBC パブリッシング

はじめに

　ラダーシリーズは、「はしご (ladder)」を使って一歩一歩上を目指すように、学習者の実力に合わせ、無理なくステップアップできるよう開発された英文リーダーのシリーズです。

　リーディング力をつけるためには、繰り返したくさん読むこと、いわゆる「多読」がもっとも効果的な学習法であると言われています。多読では、「1. 速く 2. 訳さず英語のまま 3. なるべく辞書を使わず」に読むことが大切です。スピードを計るなど、速く読むよう心がけましょう（たとえば TOEIC® テストの音声スピードはおよそ1分間に150語です）。そして1語ずつ訳すのではなく、英語を英語のまま理解するくせをつけるようにします。こうして読み続けるうちに語感がついてきて、だんだんと英語が理解できるようになるのです。まずは、ラダーシリーズの中からあなたのレベルに合った本を選び、少しずつ英文に慣れ親しんでください。たくさんの本を手にとるうちに、英文書がすらすら読めるようになってくるはずです。

《本シリーズの特徴》
- 中学校レベルから中級者レベルまで5段階に分かれています。自分に合ったレベルからスタートしてください。
- クラシックから現代文学、ノンフィクション、ビジネスと幅広いジャンルを扱っています。あなたの興味に合わせてタイトルを選べます。
- 巻末のワードリストで、いつでもどこでも単語の意味を確認できます。レベル1、2では、文中の全ての単語が、レベル3以上は中学校レベル外の単語が掲載されています。
- カバーにヘッドホーンマークのついているタイトルは、オーディオ・サポートがあります。ウェブから購入／ダウンロードし、リスニング教材としても併用できます。

《使用語彙について》

レベル1：中学校で学習する単語約1000語

レベル2：レベル1の単語＋使用頻度の高い単語約300語

レベル3：レベル1の単語＋使用頻度の高い単語約600語

レベル4：レベル1の単語＋使用頻度の高い単語約1000語

レベル5：語彙制限なし

Contents

The Human Chair *1*
Translated by Tom Christian

The Case of the Murder on D Hill *43*
Translated by Morgan Giles

Word List *108*

The Human Chair

読みはじめる前に

The Human Chair
「人間椅子」

【あらすじ】

外務省官僚を夫に持つ佳子は、毎朝、夫の登庁を見送ると、書斎へ閉じこもるのが日課だった。有名作家の彼女の元には、毎日のように読者から幾通もの手紙が届く。ある日、いつものように目を通していると、その中に「奥様」という呼びかけの言葉で始まる手紙を見つける。何気なく2行3行と読み進めていくと、そこに書かれていたのは……

【主な登場人物】

Yoshiko　佳子　美しい有名作家。ある日、「私」から手紙が届く。

I　「私」　手紙の語り手。生まれつき醜貌を持つ椅子職人。

Every morning, Yoshiko saw her husband off to work at a little after ten o'clock. It was then that she finally had some time for herself, and her habit was to shut herself up in the study—a room which she and her husband both used—in the Western-style wing of their mansion. She was currently working on a long piece of fiction for the special summer edition of K Magazine.

Famous both as a beauty and as an author, Yoshiko's reputation had grown to overshadow that of her husband, a secretary at the Foreign Office. A large number of letters from unknown admirers reached her every day.

Today, too, her first task, after sitting at her desk and before starting her work, was to cast her eye over some letters from complete strangers.

The letters all said the same dull things, as

if churned out by rote. With the considerateness and good nature typical of her sex, however, Yoshiko made a point of reading them all through, no matter how dull they were. After all, they were addressed to her.

She began with the simple-looking ones—a couple of regular letters and a post card. After she had read them, what remained was a bulky envelope; Yoshiko suspected that it contained a manuscript. Although she had not received a letter to warn her it was coming, being sent unsolicited manuscripts was nothing unusual for her. The majority were excruciatingly prolix and dull; nevertheless she tore it open and pulled out a stack of pages. "I might as well take a look at the title," she thought to herself.

Just as she had expected, it was a bound bundle of sheets of the square-printed paper favored by writers. Oddly, though, the story featured neither a title nor the name of the author, and the text began abruptly with the word "Madam," directly addressing her. "What's this?" she thought. "So it must be a letter after all." She only needed to run her eyes over the first couple of lines to see that there was something faintly abnormal, even distasteful, about the letter. But her natural curiosity soon got the better of her and she plowed ahead at high speed.

* * *

Madam,

I humbly beg your forgiveness. It is wicked for a man whom you have never even met to send you so shameless a letter, out of the blue.

No doubt, Madam, you will be taken aback when I inform you that I intend to confess to you a truly extraordinary crime that I have committed.

I can in all honesty say that for the past several months, I have been living the life of a devil, wholly hidden from the world of men. Not a soul in the wide world knows what I have been up to. Indeed, I might never have returned to the ordinary world of people, had a certain event not taken place.

Recently, however, an astonishing change of heart has taken place within me. It is that which compels me to make this confession about my unfortunate self to you. Much of what I say must strike you as suspicious; nonetheless, I beg you to read this letter through to the end. If you do so, you will understand why I feel as I do, and why I want you in particular, Madam, to hear my confession.

Where should I start? To have to recount so outlandish, so bizarre a story via so prosaic a means as a letter is embarrassing; I can barely bring myself to put pen to paper. Still, dillydallying will do me no good. What I shall do, then, is to start at the beginning and write everything down in the order in which it happened.

I am possessed of a hideously ugly appearance. Do your best to bear that in mind. Should you indulge my boldfaced request and consent to meet with me, it would be hard for me to bear your untutored response to my ugly face—now more loathsome and repulsive than ever due to months of unhealthy living.

I was born under an unlucky star. In spite of my ugly appearance, my heart has always secretly burned with unusually fierce passions. I ignored the reality—that I was no more than a simple craftsman with a face like a monster and dirt poor to boot—and was drawn to sweet dreams of luxury far beyond my social status.

Had I been born into a wealthy family, money, by enabling me to indulge in all kinds of dissipation, might have distracted me from the depressing fact of my ugliness. Had I been endowed with greater artistic talents, composing exquisite poems might have helped me forget the dreariness of life. Unlucky that I am, however, I had no such advantages. I had no choice but to earn my living as a furniture maker, one hard day at a time, doing the job that my father had passed down to me.

Making chairs of any and every kind was my specialty. Even our most demanding clients liked the chairs that I built. As a result, the company singled me out for special treatment, sending all the orders for high-quality pieces in my direction. High quality doesn't just mean carved backrests and armrests; on top of that, there were all sorts of challenging orders based on individual personal preferences about the feel of upholstery or the relative sizes of different parts of the chair. A layperson isn't equipped to imagine just how difficult these orders were to fulfill, but the pleasure of completing them was in direct proportion to the difficulty involved. Would it be presumptuous for me to compare my emotions to the joy that an artist feels upon bringing some magnificent work to completion?

Whenever I finish a chair, the first thing I do is to sit on it to see how it feels. That is the only time in my dreary artisan's life that I get to enjoy a sense of indescribable pride. What noble man or beautiful woman will sit on it next? If they were able to order so magnificent a chair, their residence must contain a sumptuous room worthy of it. Oil paintings by celebrated artists must surely line its walls and a chandelier hang from the ceiling like a magnificent jewel. Expensive carpets cover the entire floor. In front of the chair there is a table upon which sit gaudy flowers from the West, emitting a sweet scent and blooming lavishly. As I drifted deeper into my daydream, I imagined that the magnificent room belonged to me and, for the briefest of moments, felt a pleasure that surpasses my powers of description.

These ephemeral fantasies of mine grew unstoppably. Despite being a mere poor, ugly artisan, as I sat in the chair I had made myself, in the world of my dreams I was transformed into a high-minded young nobleman. To one side of me, my beautiful mistress (she always featured in my fantasies) hung on my every word, her face gleaming with smiles. Nor was that all; in my dreams, I held her hand as we whispered sweet nothings to one another.

It never took long, however, before my

dreams were interrupted by the jabbering of the local housewives and the hysterical wailing of their sickly children, and sordid reality once again exposed its grey corpse before me. Returning to reality, I was confronted with my true self: pitiably ugly and with no resemblance to a young nobleman. And as for that beautiful creature who had been smiling at me? Where had she and everything else gone? The squalid nursemaids, dusty from playing with their charges, did not so much as turn to look at me. The only thing that remained from my dream was the chair that I had made. There it stood, stolid and sad. But even it would soon be carted off who knows where to some quite different world to the one I lived in.

In this way, with every new chair I completed, an indescribable sense of life's monotony overcame me. Gradually, that ghastly—that indescribably ghastly—feeling became more than I could bear.

"If I have to live like a maggot, I'd be better off dead," I thought. And I was quite serious.

As I diligently plied my chisel, hammered in my nails or mixed up my foul-smelling paints, the same thought went around and around in my head. "Just wait a minute. If you're prepared to face death, mightn't there be another way? For instance...." My thoughts gradually began to take a fearful course.

It was precisely then that I was asked to make some large leather armchairs of a kind I had never previously put my hand to. They were destined for a hotel here in Y City that was managed by a foreign gentleman. They were the kind of thing he would normally have ordered from his home country, but the company for which I worked had managed to win the order by convincing him that craftsmen existed in Japan who were capable of making chairs that were not inferior to those from abroad. That was enough to inspire me: I forgot about the comforts of life and got to work. I toiled obsessively, putting my heart and soul into the job.

Looking at the finished chairs, I felt an

unprecedented sense of satisfaction. Though I say it myself, they displayed marvelous and eye-catching workmanship. As was my habit, I dragged one of the four chairs into a wooden-floored room that got plenty of sunshine and plopped myself luxuriantly down. Sitting on it felt wonderful! The pressure of the cushioning—plump but neither too hard nor too soft; the touch of the untreated leather (which I had opted not to dye, leaving it a natural color) against the skin; the opulent backrest, tilted at just the right angle to support the back; the two richly bulbous armrests with their delicate curves: They were all in perfect accord and struck as the physical expression of the phrase "harmonious comfort."

I was in ecstasy as I sank deep into the chair and squeezed the plump round armrests. Then, as was always the case with me, a series of fantasies spontaneously bubbled unstoppably up, as vivid and as colorful as the many-colored rainbow. They unfurled in front of my eyes, so clear and so true to my imagination, that I feared that I was losing my mind.

The Human Chair

As this was going on, a wonderful idea suddenly occurred to me. (I wonder if this is what people mean when they talk about "the devil whispering in one's ear"?) It was as fantastic as a dream and exceedingly perverse. But that very perversity gave it an indescribable appeal which I just could not resist.

At the beginning, it was no more than a simple wish not to let go of the beautiful chair which I had worked so hard on; if I could, I wanted to accompany it wherever it went. As the wish slowly and hypnotically grew inside me, at some point it attached itself to an appalling project that had been festering in my mind lately. Oh, I must be quite mad, for I resolved to put my utterly freakish fantasy into action.

I hastily disassembled the handsomest of the four armchairs I had made, then rebuilt it in such a way that I could realize my bizarre plan.

It was an exceptionally large armchair, so the leather-covered base on which you sit almost reached the floor, while the backrest and the arms were unusually broad. Inside it there was a hollow space that ran through the whole thing, such that a man could hide himself in it with no risk of being detected. In this space, I had, of course, installed a sturdy wooden frame and a large number of springs, but a little clever workmanship was all it took for me to create a cavity that was big enough to hide in, provided you sat following the shape of the chair, with your lap beneath the seat and your head and upper body in the backrest.

Since clever adjustments of this kind are my forte, I found it easy enough to reconfigure the chair in a skillful manner. For instance, I made a slit in the leather—quite invisible from the outside—that enabled me to breathe and hear what was going on around me; inside the backrest, right by where my head would be, I also constructed a little shelf for storage and stocked it with a water bottle and some army hardtack. I equipped myself with a large rubber bag for certain basic physical needs and came up with various other contrivances, such that, provided I had food, I could stay inside for two or three days without experiencing any inconvenience. The chair now had become a room just right for one person, you might say.

Stripping down to my undershirt, I opened the flap that I had built into the bottom of the chair, and slid inside. It felt strange, I must admit. Pitch dark, hard to breathe, just like being in a tomb—all in all an extraordinary sensation. Come to think of it, it really was like the tomb: the instant that I entered the chair, I had vanished from the world of men, as if I had donned a cloak of invisibility.

A few moments later, one of my fellow employees came around; he was pushing a big handcart to collect the four armchairs. My apprentice—the two of us lived together by ourselves—welcomed him, oblivious as to what was going on. As the laborers loaded up the handcart, one of them growled, "This damn thing weighs a ton!" Inside the chair, I couldn't help giving a start. Still, given that armchairs tend to be heavy things anyway, no one was unduly suspicious and in due course I felt a strange sensation as the thunderous rattling of the cart was transmitted through me.

I was exceedingly anxious; in the end, though, nothing untoward happened, and the chair with me in it was deposited with a heavy thump in one of the rooms in the hotel that afternoon. It was only later that I found out that this was not a guest bedroom, but a place called a "lounge" where people meet, peruse the newspapers, and smoke cigarettes, with a great variety of characters always coming and going.

I imagine that you have already divined the chief purpose of this eccentric endeavor of mine: to keep watch until no one was about, then to slip out of my chair and prowl around the hotel stealing things. After all, who on earth would ever think of anything so ludicrous as a person hiding in a chair! Like a shadow, I was able to break into one room after another completely at will. As

soon as people began to raise a rumpus, I would scoot back to my hidey-hole inside the chair and, taking care to breathe as quietly as I could, amuse myself by watching their nincompoopish attempts to find me. Have you heard of the hermit crab? It's a species of crab that lives on the beach right where the waves break. It looks like a large spider and it struts about as if it owns the place when there's no one nearby. The instant it detects the faintest of footsteps, however, it withdraws into its shell with an extraordinary turn of speed. Then, with just the tiniest length of its disgusting hairy forelegs sticking out of its shell, it watches the movements of its enemy. I was exactly like one of those hermit crabs. My hiding place was a chair rather than a shell, and I swaggered around the hotel rather than a beach.

Anyway, this outlandish plan of mine, precisely because it was so outlandish, caught everyone off guard and was a marvelous success. By my third day at the hotel, I had already accomplished a great deal. The fear-tinged yet enjoyable feeling that accompanies the carrying out of a robbery, and the indescribable thrill when you manage to pull it off; the amusement to be derived from silently watching people making a commotion right in front of you—"*He went this-a-way!*" "*No, he went that-a-way*": Well, you can probably imagine the extraordinary charm it had for me, and how much entertainment I derived from it.

Unfortunately, though, I do not now have the time to go into such matters in detail. Because this was when I stumbled upon a preeminently bizarre form of pleasure that delighted me ten—nay, twenty—times as much as stealing things. Revealing that to you is the true purpose of this letter.

I need to go back to the beginning and start my story from when my chair was deposited in the hotel lounge.

When the chair was delivered, the hotel managers spent a while testing it for comfort; then everything went quiet; I couldn't hear a thing. I suspect that the room was deserted. Nonetheless, for a while after my arrival, I was far too frightened to emerge from the chair. For an extremely long time (or perhaps it just felt that way to me) I strained my ears, listening intently to catch any sounds so I could form an idea of what was going on around me.

After a while, I heard the thump-thump-thump (I think it came from the corridor) of someone walking with a heavy tread. The sound came to within five or six yards of me, then became almost inaudible due to the carpet on the floor. A moment later, I heard a man's rough nasal breathing, and before I could even get over my surprise, a large man—it had to be a Westerner—plunked himself down on my lap, then bounced lightly up and down a couple of times. With only a single strip of leather separating my thighs from his magnificent burly buttocks, I was so close that I could feel his bodily warmth. His broad shoulders leaned right up against my chest and his weighty arms overlay mine through the leather. I suppose he must have lit a cigar, for a rich male fragrance came wafting through the slit in the leather.

Try, Madam, to put yourself in my shoes and imagine what is was like. What a truly amazing scene it was! Overcome with terror, I am tightly scrunched up in the darkness within the chair, cold sweat pouring from my armpits; the power of thought deserts me; I drift into a stupor.

That man was only the first; throughout the day all sorts of people took turns to sit upon my lap. Not one of them had the least inkling that I was in there or that what they took for comfortable upholstery was in fact a living pair of human thighs.

It was a leather-sheathed world, pitch dark and permitting no movement. Can you imagine how mysterious, yet how appealing a world it was? In it, one perceived human beings as extraordinary creatures, utterly different to the people one sees around one on a daily basis. They are reduced to their voices, their breathing, their footsteps, the rustle of their clothes and a few round, springy lumps of flesh. And I can distinguish them not by their appearance, but by their feel. Someone grossly fat feels like a putrid fish. Contrarily, a gaunt, shriveled person feels like a skeleton. The bend of their spine, the spread of their shoulder blades, the length of their arms, the meatiness of their thighs, the protuberance of their tail bone—take all these together and there is always something different about people, no matter how similar their physiques. There is no doubt that one can identify people based on their overall feel, as well as on their facial appearance and their fingerprints.

The same can also be said about the opposite sex. While under normal circumstances we evaluate them largely based on their looks, that is out of the question in the world within the chair. All you have to go on is their bare flesh, the tone of their voice and their scent.

I hope, Madam, that you will not be offended at the frankness of my account, but it was in the lobby that I developed a powerful physical attachment to a woman. (She was the first woman to ever sit on my chair.)

If I try to picture her based on the sound of her voice, she would be a rather young girl from somewhere abroad. She came in when there was no one else in the room, half-dancing and singing an extraordinary song under her breath as if she had just received some good news. No sooner had I sensed that she was standing in front of the chair in which I was hidden than she flung her voluptuous yet supremely supple body right on top of me. Something must have struck her as funny, for she burst into peals of laughter and clapped her hands and stamped her feet, bouncing around as vigorously as a fish caught in a net.

For almost a full half hour, she sat on my knees, occasionally breaking into song and wiggling her heavy figure in time to the music.

To be honest, this unforeseen experience was an earth-shattering event for me. Having regarded women as sacred beings (or maybe

more as frightening ones), I had never had the courage to even look at their faces. Now I, of all people, was so close to this unknown foreign girl—not just in the same room and in the same chair, but able to feel the warmth of her skin through a single thin strip of leather. For her part, she felt no awkwardness and was happy to consign her full weight to my knees and behave with the easy-going lack of inhibition that comes from thinking oneself unobserved. I could make as if to hug her from within the chair. Through the leather I could kiss the luscious nape of her neck. I was at complete liberty to do whatever I wanted with her.

As a result of my making this startling discovery, my original goal of theft took a back seat; I was now utterly infatuated with the wonderful world of sensation. I even convinced myself that the within-a-chair world was my naturally ordained habitat. A worthless fellow like me—ugly, weak-willed, tormented by a sense of inferiority—could only live a life of shame and misery in the bright and cheery world outside. Now, by simply changing the environment in which I lived, provided I could endure the cramped conditions within my chair, I could get close to beautiful people—hear their voices, touch their bodies—who would never allow me to approach them, let alone speak to them in the bright world outside.

Love inside a chair! It is impossible for anyone who has not actually climbed into a chair to imagine how extraordinary and intoxicating a charm it holds. It is a love comprised only of touch, hearing and a little bit of smell. It is the love of a world of darkness. It is certainly not a love of this world. Perhaps it is the lecherous lust of the devil's own domain. When you stop to think about it, all the aberrant and terrifying things that take place in the nooks and crannies beyond people's notice are truly mind-boggling!

My original plan had been to slip out of the hotel as soon as I had done the stealing I had set out to do; in thrall, however, as I was to a most bizarre form of pleasure, far from getting out of the place, I persisted with my new way of living, resolved to make the interior of the chair my permanent home.

My nightly expeditions involved no danger as I took the utmost care neither to make a sound nor to be seen by anyone. Nonetheless, the fact that I could live inside the chair for several whole months without even coming close to detection came as a surprise even to me.

I was spending almost all day, every day in the cramped interior of the chair with my arms and my legs bent. Numb all over and unable to stand upright as a result, I was reduced to scuttling to and fro the kitchen and the bathroom like a crab. I must be insane! For despite all the discomfort I had to endure, I just could not see my way to abandoning that wonderful world of sensation.

For a few of the guests, the hotel was more like a home and they stayed there for a month, sometimes two; still, given the nature of hotels, the majority of people were always coming or going. In consequence, I just had to accept that the objects of my abnormal affections would change as time went by. The memory of my many mistresses was graven in my heart not according to what they looked like, as per the normal way, but primarily according to their physical shape.

One girl was lean and slender and fearless as a filly. Wriggling and writhing wantonly, another had the allure of a snake. Yet another, lavishly endowed with springy fat, was plump as a rubber ball. Another, her body perfectly developed, was hard and strong as a Greek sculpture. Every woman's body had its own distinct charm.

As I switched like this from one woman to the next, I got to enjoy other extraordinary experiences, of a quite different kind.

One of these involved the ambassador of a Great European Power (I discovered his rank from the gossiping of the Japanese bellboy) who, on one occasion, reposed his noble form upon my lap. Already well known as a politician, he also had a worldwide reputation as a poet. That was reason enough for the opportunity to feel the skin of this great man to give me a thrill of pride. As he sat on top of me, he conducted a roughly ten-minute-long conversation with several of his countrymen before rising to his feet. I didn't, of course, have the faintest idea what he was talking about, but every time he made a gesture, his whole body (which seemed warmer to me than that of the average person) shifted ponderously, galvanizing me in a manner that defies description.

That was when an idea suddenly popped into my head. What sort of effect would I provoke if I made a single deep thrust with a sharp dagger through the leather straight at his heart? It would certainly cause a fatal wound from which he would not recover. What sort of brouhaha would be enacted not just in his home country, but in Japanese political circles? What sort of impassioned articles would the newspapers run about the event? For sure, his death would be a serious loss for the world, having a serious impact on diplomatic relations between Japan and his country, not to mention from an artistic perspective. With a simple action on my part, I could easily make this grave incident into a reality. At the thought, I could not help feeling quite extraordinarily pleased with myself.

Another episode involved a famous dancer who came to Japan and happened to stay in this hotel and—it was only the one time—sat upon my chair. On that occasion, I felt as moved as I had with the ambassador, but in addition, the dancer transmitted to me a sensation of ideal physical beauty that I had never felt before. So overpowering was her beauty that there was no room in my mind for vulgar thoughts; instead I adored her with the reverence one might direct toward a work of art.

I had many other bizarre, marvelous or perverse experiences. To detail them, however, is not the purpose of this letter, which is already rather on the long side. I should hurry up and get to the main point.

Several months after I had gotten to the hotel, a change took place in my circumstances. For some reason, the hotel manager had to return to his native country and the hotel was made over as a going concern to a Japanese-run company. Abandoning the hotel's original luxury orientation, the Japanese company planned to make the business more profitable by running it as more of a mass-market, Japanese-style inn. As a result, such furniture as was no longer needed was handed over to a big furniture dealer to be auctioned off. My chair was one of the items to be featured in the auction catalogue.

My first reaction on hearing the news was disappointment. Then I began to think I could use it as an opportunity to return to "the outside" and start life anew. By then, the money I had stolen amounted to a considerable sum, so even if I rejoined the world, I would not have to live the same miserable life as before.

Looking back at it now, leaving the foreign-run hotel was a big disappointment in one way, but a new source of hope in another. Let me explain: Despite having fallen in love with such a variety of women over several months, I could not help feeling that something was lacking on the emotional side, because my female counterparts—regardless how splendid and pleasing their physical attributes—were all foreigners. When push comes to shove, surely a Japanese cannot feel genuine love unless it is toward another Japanese? That was the way my thoughts were tending when my chair was put up for auction. "Perhaps I'll be acquired by a Japanese person. Maybe I'll find a place in a Japanese family." That was my latest aspiration. The upshot was that I decided to continue with my life inside the chair for a little while longer.

I had a dreadful time for several days in the furniture dealer's store. Luckily, though, once the auction got under way, my chair was quick to find a buyer. Although it was now second-hand, the chair was still sufficiently splendid to attract notice.

The Human Chair

The buyer was a civil servant who lived in the metropolis not all that far from Y City. Being transported inside the chair on a ferociously shaking truck for many miles from the furniture shop to his residence was so uncomfortable, I thought I was going to die. Still, my discomfort barely deserves a mention in light of the joy I felt at my buyer being, as I had hoped, Japanese.

My civil servant purchaser was the owner of a truly splendid mansion. My chair was deposited in a large study in its Western-style wing. What gave me enormous satisfaction was the fact that the study was used less by the husband and more by his young and beautiful wife. Since arriving here, I have spent roughly a month constantly in her company. Other than when she is eating or sleeping, her supple body is always on top of me. You see, she is always in the study, absorbed in her writing.

This is not the place for me to go on at length about how deeply I fell for her. Not only was she the first Japanese woman I had gotten close to, she was also the possessor of a more than beautiful body. I was truly in love for the first time in my life. In comparison, my many experiences at the hotel were undeserving of the name. The proof of that is, I believe, clear—for with her, I felt something I had never felt before: enjoying secret caresses was no longer adequate and I went to considerable trouble to make her aware of my presence.

If possible, I wanted her to sense that I was inside the chair. And then—I know I'm pushing my luck here—I wanted her to fall in love with me. How could I get that across to her? If I just told her straight out that there was a person hiding inside the chair, she would be sure to tell her husband and the servants out of sheer shock. That would ruin everything; worse, I would also face charges for a heinous crime and be liable for punishment under the law.

I decided that my best bet was to try to make her feel so comfortable in my chair that she developed an affection for it. Artist that she was, she was sure to have a finer sensibility than average. If I could get her to sense the life in my chair and make her love it as a living creature rather than an inanimate object, that would be satisfaction enough for me.

When she flung herself down on top of me, I tried to receive her as softly and gently as I could. When she was sitting on me and was tired, I would slowly and imperceptibly shift my legs to adjust her position. Then, when she finally dozed off and slept, I would play the part of a cradle, jiggling my knees lightly up and down.

I could just be imagining things, but recently I think that my thoughtfulness has been rewarded; the woman seems to have developed a fondness for the chair. She lowers herself into it with the tender sweetness of a baby nestling in its mother's bosom or of a young girl receiving her lover's embrace. I can also detect a sentimental wistfulness in the way she moves upon my lap.

Thus it was that my passion burned more fiercely with every passing day. Until finally—Ah, Madam!—until finally, I ended up wishing for something so outrageous as to overstep all bounds of propriety: *If I could just catch just a glimpse of my beloved's face and exchange a word or two with her, I would be happy to die.* That was how far my obsessive thoughts went.

Of course, Madam, I know that you have already figured it out. Forgive my insolence in using the phrase "my lover." The truth is, I mean you. I am the pitiful man who has been so devotedly but hopelessly in love with you ever since your husband purchased my chair at that furniture shop in Y City.

This, Madam, is my dearest wish. Could you not possibly meet with me just once? Could you not then offer a single word of comfort to this pitiable and ugly man? Believe me, I will not ask for more. I am too hideous, too morally tainted to entertain such a hope. I beg you, please, please indulge the ardent prayer of an utterly unhappy man.

The Human Chair

I slipped out of your mansion to write this letter last night. Not only would it be very risky for me to make this request face to face, Madam, I simply cannot bring myself to do so.

As you read this letter, I am hovering just outside your house, pale with anxiety.

If you are prepared to grant my most impertinent request, kindly place your handkerchief over the pot of fringed pinks in the window. I shall respond to your signal by going up to the front door of your house, like any ordinary visitor.

* * *

This passionate prayer brought the whole extraordinary letter to an end.

Such were Yoshiko's fearful forebodings that by the time she was halfway through it, the blood had quite drained from her face.

Hardly aware of what she was doing, she sprang to her feet and fled from the study with the horrible chair to the living room in the Japanese part of the house. She thought about ripping up the letter and throwing it away without reading it through, but curiosity got the upper hand and she kept on reading at the low desk in the living room.

Her fears were justified.

The thought of it was just too terrifying! *A complete and utter stranger had been inside the armchair in which she sat every day of the week.*

"How disgusting!"

She shuddered as though someone had splashed cold water down her back. The trembling would not stop, but went on, seemingly without end.

It was too much to take in. Yoshiko was stupefied; she had no idea what to do. Should she try examining the chair? Could she really bring herself to do something so repulsive? Although the man was no longer inside it,

there were sure to be food scraps and other filthy residues of his left behind.

"Madam, a letter for you."

Yoshiko gave a start. Turning, she saw one of the maids bearing a letter which, she said, had just been delivered.

Yoshiko took it automatically; she was just about to open it, when she noticed the inscription and dropped the letter, struck by the most violent and awful surprise. *Her name was in the same hand as the foul letter she had just finished reading!*

For a long time, she could not make up her mind whether or not to open the letter. In the end, she ripped off the seal and read it, her nerves jangling all the while. Although extremely short, the letter was strange enough to give her yet another jolt.

* * *

Once again, I must beg your forgiveness for so rudely sending you this letter with no sort of overture. I have been an enthusiastic reader of your masterful work for the longest time. The letter I sent under separate cover was my clumsy attempt at fiction. I would be thrilled if you could look it over and give me your opinion. For reasons of my own, I sent you the manuscript before writing this letter, so I assume that you have already read it. What did you think of it? Nothing would give me greater pleasure than the news that my modest little piece of fiction managed to make an impression upon a master of the art such as yourself.

I deliberately left the title off the manuscript; I am thinking of calling the story "The Human Chair."

With apologies for my rudeness. Sincerely and gratefully yours.

The Case of
the Murder on D Hill

読みはじめる前に

The Case of the Murder on D Hill
「D坂の殺人事件」

【あらすじ】

九月初旬のある蒸し暑い晩のこと。D坂の大通りにあるカフェ「白梅軒」にいた「私」は、知り合いの明智小五郎と共に、カフェの向かいにある古本屋で起きた殺人事件の第一発見者となる。侵入経路も犯人も見えてこない実に不可解なこの事件について、「私」と明智はそれぞれ推理するが……

【主な登場人物】

I　私　物語の語り手。学校を出たばかりの下宿人。探偵趣味がある。

Akechi Kogoro　明智小五郎　煙草屋の二階に下宿している風変わりな男。探偵小説好き。

the wife of the bookstore　古本屋の細君　明智の幼馴染。全身傷だらけの絞殺死体となって発見される。

It was a sultry night in early September. I was sipping an iced coffee at the White Plum Blossom Café, a place I often went to near the middle of the main road on D Hill. At the time, I had just left school and had no work to speak of; I spent my days lazing around my boarding house reading books, and when I tired of that, I would go out on aimless walks, making the rounds of cafés that did not cost too much. This was my daily routine. The White Plum Blossom Café was not far from my boarding house, and it was situated such that wherever I walked to I would always pass by it, so it was the café I went to most, but I had the bad habit of lingering too long in any café I entered. And since I have always had a small appetite and little in my purse, I would have two or three cups of cheap coffee and take an hour or two over them, not ordering even one dish of food. Still, it was not that I particularly had taken a liking to any of the waitresses or wanted to harass them. It was better at any rate than my boarding house, and more cheerful. That night I was, as usual, taking my time drinking a cup of iced coffee while stationed at my usual table facing the road, staring absentmindedly out the window.

Now, D Hill, where the White Plum Blossom Café was located and which was previously known for chrysanthemum dolls, had just had its narrow street widened into a broad road called Something Mile Road as part of the urban renewal projects of the Taisho Era, so here and there on both sides of the street were still some empty lots, and at the time of this story it was much lonelier than it is now. Across the road, directly opposite the White Plum Blossom Café, there was a used bookstore. Actually, I had been staring at this storefront for quite some time. As a shabby bookstore on the outskirts of town it was not much to look at, but I had a bit of a special interest in it. That is to say, I had heard from a strange man I had met recently in the White Plum Blossom Café—a man by the name of

The Case of the Murder on D Hill

Akechi Kogoro, an exceedingly odd man to speak to; he seemed intelligent, but the thing which had charmed me about him was his love of detective novels—that a woman who had been his childhood friend was now the wife of the owner of this bookstore. According to the memories I had of buying books there two or three times, the wife of the bookstore owner was quite a beauty, and although I could not put my finger on what it was exactly, there was something sensual about her which was attractive to men. She was always in charge of the store at night and should have been that night as well, but despite the shop being a small one with only half-width frontage, I looked for her and saw nobody there. Certain that she would come out soon, I waited, watching patiently.

But she did not emerge. Tiring of this, I decided to shift my gaze to the watchmaker's next door. This is when I suddenly noticed that the paper sliding doors with lattice windows that separated the store and the inner rooms were shut tightly. (These sliding doors were of the type which specialists refer to as *muso*, meaning that the central portion which normally would have paper pasted over it was instead made into a narrow, vertical double lattice which could be opened and closed.) Well, that was rather odd indeed. Places like bookstores are very susceptible to shoplifters, so the lattice allowed people inside to keep watch even when they were not in charge of the store, which made it quite strange that the lattice was closed. Had it been cold that would be understandable, but it was barely the beginning of September and the night was so sultry that to have those doors closed was odd. As these thoughts went through my mind, I realized it was likely something was going on in the inner rooms, and I did not feel like turning my gaze away any longer.

Speaking of the bookstore owner's wife, I had once heard the waitresses in that café sharing a strange rumor. Although it was just part of their inventory of the ladies and girls they saw in the bathhouse, what I heard them say was: "The mistress of the bookstore is a very pretty lady, but when she's naked, her whole body is covered in bruises—obviously the marks of being beaten and pinched. Her marriage doesn't seem especially bad, either—how strange!" At this point, another woman joined in. "And the mistress of the *soba* place a few doors down, Asahiya, is often bruised, too. Hers are clearly from being beaten, as well." Now, I did not stop to consider deeply what that bit of gossip might mean, only thinking how cruel their husbands must be, but dear readers, that was not the case at all. Only later did I understand that this trifling matter had an important connection to this whole story.

At any rate, I stared for over half an hour at the same place. Perhaps you could say it was a premonition, but somehow, I felt that something might happen while I was looking on, and I could not turn my eyes away no matter what. At that moment, Akechi Kogoro, whose name I just mentioned, walked past the window, wearing the same bold, broad-striped *yukata* as always and swinging his shoulders strangely as he walked. Noticing me, he nodded in greeting and came inside. He ordered a cold coffee and sat down next to me facing the window just as I was. Then, realizing that I was looking at one place, he followed my gaze and looked at the same secondhand bookstore opposite. And, curiously, he also seemed truly interested. He stared in that direction without moving his eyes even a little.

While we stared at the same place as if by arrangement, we exchanged all sorts of small talk. As I have now already forgotten what topics we discussed then, and as our conversation has no real connection to the story at hand, I will simply say that I am certain our conversation involved crime and detectives. I will attempt to reproduce a sample of our conversation:

"It should be impossible to commit a crime that cannot be uncovered, shouldn't it? But I think it is quite possible. Look at Tanizaki Jun'ichiro's *On the Road*. There's no way to detect a crime like that. Of course, in that novel, a detective does discover it, but that was an invention thanks to the author's tremendous power of imagination," said Akechi.

"No, I don't think so. Practical considerations aside, logically speaking, there is no such thing as a crime that cannot be solved. The only thing is, there's no detective on the police force now as great as the one in *On the Road*," I said.

It was that sort of thing. But at one point, we both fell silent as if we had planned it that way. For some time as we had talked, something interesting had been happening at the used bookstore opposite which we had kept our eyes on.

"So you noticed it too," I whispered, and he replied immediately.

"The book thieves, you mean? Very odd, isn't it? I've been watching them since I came in here. This must be the fourth one."

"You haven't even been here half an hour yet, and there have been four thieves—it is a bit strange. I've been looking over there since before you came in. It was about an hour ago; do you see those sliding doors? I noticed that the lattice part was closed, and I've been paying attention ever since."

"Haven't the people who live there gone out then?"

"But those doors haven't opened even once. If they went out I suppose they could have gone out the back door.... But it is decidedly strange that no one's been there for over half an hour. How about it? Shall we go over there?"

"Yes, let's. Even if nothing bad is going on inside the house, perhaps something else has happened in the store."

I left the café, thinking how interesting it would be if this was a criminal incident. I am sure that Akechi was thinking the very same thing. He, too, was more than a little excited.

The bookstore was of a common type, with a dirt floor throughout the store, bookshelves on the left and far wall stretching nearly from floor to ceiling, with platforms for displaying books at bench height. In the middle of the dirt floor, like an island, there was a rectangular platform for stacking up and displaying books. And just three feet from the right of the bookshelf on the far wall was the passageway to the inner rooms, with the paper door I mentioned earlier. Usually, the master or mistress of the store would be sitting on the *tatami* mat in front of this door, keeping watch.

Akechi and I walked toward this *tatami* mat and called out loudly, but there was no reply. It seemed there was no one there. I slid the door open a little and peered inside. The electric light was off and it was pitch black, but a vaguely human form seemed to be lying in the corner. Thinking this was suspicious, I again called out, but they did not answer.

"What the hell, we might as well go in."

So the two of us stepped inside noisily. Akechi twisted the switch for the electric light. At that moment, we both shouted, "Ah!" at the same time. In the corner of the now-bright room lay a woman's corpse.

"It's the mistress of the store," I said eventually. "It looks like she's been strangled, doesn't it?"

Akechi went to her side and examined the body. "There's no chance of resuscitating her at all. We'd better let the police know quickly. I'll go to the public telephone. You keep watch. It would be better if the neighborhood wasn't alerted yet. We mustn't let any clues get destroyed, after all."

Leaving me with these orders, he dashed off to the public telephone, which was located just half a block away.

Although I could hold my own well in an argument about crime or detectives, this was my first time to be confronted with either in reality. I could not do anything. All there was for me to do was just look around the room intently.

The room was a single six-mat room, and further inside on the right, a narrow porch separated it from the lavatory and a garden no more than sixty-four square feet, with a wooden fence at the back of the garden. (The porch had been left open because it was summer, so I had a clear view.) On the left side of the room was a hinged door, and beyond that was a wood-floored room about two mats in size where I could see a small bathing area next to the back door, a tall paneled wooden door which was closed. On the right side opposite this, there were four sliding screens which were open, and beyond that were the stairs to the second floor and a storeroom. This arrangement was a common one for a cheap row house.

The corpse was near the left wall, lying with her head facing toward the store. To avoid disturbing the scene of the crime, and partly because I felt uneasy, I decided not to approach the body. But the room was small, and as I kept watch, my eyes naturally went in that direction. The woman wore a rough

yukata with a *chuugata* pattern and lay almost facing upward. Although her clothes were pulled up over her knees, high enough to show her thighs, there were no particular signs of a struggle. I do not know much about these things, but it appeared that her neck was turning purple where she had been strangled.

There was no end to the people passing by on the road outside. Life went on peacefully and without incident—people talked loudly, their *geta* clapping as they walked, and some drunkenly sang popular songs. Inside the house behind a set of paper doors, a woman had been brutally murdered and lay dead. How ironic. I became strangely sentimental and stood there in a daze.

"They'll be here soon," said Akechi, who was out of breath.

"Right."

Even speaking had become somehow difficult for me. The two of us looked at each other for a long time without speaking a word.

Before long, a policeman in uniform arrived along with a man in a suit. The uniformed man, I later learned, was the chief inspector of K Police Station, and the other man, as one could see from his appearance and what he carried, was a medical officer connected to the same station. We gave the chief inspector a rough explanation of the situation from the beginning. Then, I added this:

"When Akechi here entered the café, I happened to look at the clock. It was precisely half past eight, so I believe the lattice in these doors was probably closed around eight. At that time the electric light inside was definitely on. So it is clear that around eight, at least, there was some living person in this room."

While the chief inspector listened to our statement and took it down in his notebook, the medical officer finished his preliminary examination of the corpse. He waited for us to pause and then he spoke.

"Strangulation. It was done by hand. Take a

look at this. Where the skin is turning purple, those are fingerprints. And where she is bleeding is where the fingernails were. Looking at this thumbprint on the right side of her neck, we can see that it was done with a right hand. Let me see... what else? She hasn't been dead for more than an hour, I'd say. But of course, it is too late for resuscitation."

"She appears to have been held down from above," said the chief inspector thoughtfully. "But even so, there's no sign of a struggle.... It must have been done terribly suddenly. And with incredible strength."

Then, he turned toward us and asked us what had happened to the master of the house. But of course, we had no way of knowing. So Akechi, sensibly, called for the owner of the watch store next door.

The chief inspector's questions and the watch store owner's answers went largely as follows.

"Do you know where the master went to?"

"The master of this store goes out every night to sell books at the night markets, and he usually doesn't come home until around midnight, sir."

"Where are these night markets he sells at?"

"I understand he often goes to Hirokoji in Ueno. As for where he went tonight, unfortunately, I do not know, sir."

"You didn't hear any sounds here an hour ago, did you?"

"What do you mean by 'sounds'?"

"You know what I mean. Like this woman crying out when she was killed, or the sound of a scuffle...."

"I am afraid I did not hear any sounds of that kind."

As this was happening, people in the neighborhood got word and started gathering, and along with curious onlookers who had been passing by, the front of the used bookstore was thronged with people. Among them was also the lady from the *tabi* store on the other side of the bookstore, there to back up the man from the watch shop. She also stated that she had heard no sounds at all.

During all this, the people of the neighborhood, after consulting amongst themselves, had sent a messenger to where the master of the bookstore was.

Thereupon, I heard a car stop out front and a number of people clomped in to the store. There was a group from the prosecutor's office who had come running because of an urgent message from the police, as well as the chief of K Police Station and Detective Kobayashi, widely reputed as a famous detective then, all of whom had arrived at the same time. (These details and many others I learned afterward, of course, because a friend of mine who was a court reporter was on very friendly terms with Kobayashi, the detective in charge of this case.) The chief inspector, having arrived first, explained the situation so far to these people.

We also had to repeat our statements one more time.

"Close the front door."

Suddenly, a man in a black alpaca jacket and white trousers, who looked like a low-level company employee, shouted this order and the door was closed swiftly. This was Detective Kobayashi. Having repelled the rubberneckers thusly, he set upon his investigation. His manner was tremendously arrogant, and he behaved as if the prosecutor and the chief were not there at all. From beginning to end he acted alone. He acted as if the others were mere onlookers, who had come to stand by and watch his deft actions. First, he examined the body. He was especially careful as he turned her neck.

"These finger marks have nothing particularly distinguishing about them. In short, there is also no evidence that anything happened here other than an ordinary human pressing her down with his right hand."

He looked at the prosecutor as he spoke. Next, he suggested temporarily stripping the body. For that, we observers had to be expelled into the shop, as if it were a secret meeting of the Diet. Because of that, I am not certain what was discovered during that time, but in my judgment they must have taken note of the numerous fresh wounds on the deceased's body. These would be the ones the waitresses in the café had been gossiping about.

At last the secret meeting was dismissed, but we refrained from entering the inner room, peering in from the aforementioned *tatami* mat that divided the shop floor and the back. Fortunately, as we were the people who had discovered the incident and additionally because they later had to take Akechi's fingerprints, we were not ejected until the end. Perhaps the correct way to put it is that we were being detained. But because Detective Kobayashi's activities were not just limited to the back room but had a wide range including the outdoors, we had no way to tell the pattern of his investigation from where we stood waiting in one spot. However, luckily for us, the prosecutor camped out in the inner room and barely moved from beginning to end, so as the detectives came and went we got to listen to each of them report on the findings of their investigation without missing out on anything. The prosecutor had his clerk write up the makings of a record on the basis of these reports.

Firstly, a search of the inner room where the body was located had been carried out, but no personal items, footprint, or anything else had caught the detectives' eyes. There was only one exception.

"There are fingerprints on the switch for the electric light," said the detective, sprinkling some kind of white powder on the black Ebonite switch. "Considering the order of the circumstances, whoever turned off the light must have been the culprit. But which one of you turned it on?"

Akechi replied that it had been he.

"I see. Please let us take your fingerprints

later. Take care not to touch the electric light; we'll dismount it to take with us."

Then, the detective went up to the second floor and did not come back down for a while, but when he did come down, he went outside immediately saying he needed to take a look at the alley. That took him perhaps ten minutes. In good time he returned, the flashlight in his hand still on, bringing with him a man. He was a filthy man, barely forty, dressed in a dirty crepe shirt and khaki trousers.

"There's almost no point looking for footprints," the detective reported. "Near this back door there is an awful lot of mud because it gets very little sun, and it is a jumble of *geta* tracks, so it is very difficult to untangle the situation. By the way, this man," he said, pointing at the man he had just brought with him, "runs an ice cream store on the corner where this alley comes out. The alley has one outlet, so if the culprit did run out the back, this man must have seen him. You, answer my questions once more."

Thereafter, the ice cream man was questioned by the detective.

"Did anyone come or go down this alley around eight o'clock tonight?"

"Not one person, and since it became dark, not so much as a kitten has passed by here." The ice cream man was rather good at answering to the point.

"I've been running a shop here for a long time, and even the ladies in these row houses rarely go through here at night. Anyway, the alley takes you through places with bad footing, and it's pitch black."

"Did any of the customers of your shop go into the alley?"

"No, they did not. Everyone ate their ice cream in front of me and went straight back the way they came. Of that I am certain."

Well, if the testimony of this ice cream man was to be trusted, even if the culprit had run off through the back door of the house, he did not come out of the alley which was the only path from the back door. That said, he hadn't gone out through the front either, because we had been watching it from the White Plum Blossom Café. So what precisely had happened to him? According to Detective Kobayashi's thinking, either the culprit could have been hiding out in one of the row houses which lined both sides of the alley, or one of the tenants was the culprit. Although there was a way to escape along the roofs from the second story, upon investigation of the second story the front windows had lattices fitted which did not seem to have been moved in the slightest. The windows at the back of all the houses on the second floor were left open in that heat, and inside were people hanging up their washing, so it seemed that it would have been a little difficult to escape that way. So that was that.

The investigators had a consultation amongst themselves about how to proceed with their investigation, and eventually they decided to split up and go door to door through the area. I say that, but there were only eleven houses on either side of the alley, so it was not much trouble for them. At the same time, the interior of the house was examined again from underneath the porch up to the eaves, in every nook and cranny. But not only did this not bear any fruit, it rather appeared to complicate matters. That is to say, it was found that the owner of the confectionary store next to the used bookstore had been up on his roof where clothes were set to dry, playing his *shakuhachi* from sunset until a few moments ago, and from beginning to end he had been sitting in a position where he could not have failed to see anything that happened with the windows on the second story of the used bookstore.

Dear readers, the case had become quite interesting. Where had the culprit come in, and from where had he escaped? It could not have been by the back door, it could not have been by the second-story windows, and it could not have been by the front, of course. Had he not existed from the beginning, or had he disappeared like smoke? And these were not the only mysteries. A pair of students that Detective Kobayashi brought in front of the prosecutor gave truly strange statements. They were students at a technical school who were renting one of the row houses behind the store, and neither of them appeared to be the kind of man to talk nonsense, but nonetheless their statements were of such a nature that they made the incident more and more inexplicable.

In response to the prosecutor's questions, their answers were roughly as follows.

"Around eight o'clock, I was standing in the front of this used bookstore and I had opened up a magazine on that table and was looking at it. Then, because I heard a noise from the back, I suddenly looked up toward these *shoji*, but they had been closed. However, this lattice-like part was open, so through the gap I could see a man standing there. But just as I raised my eyes the man shut the lattice, so of course I cannot give more details, however I am certain that it was a man because of his belt."

"Did you notice anything else about him, other than that he was a man? His height, or the pattern of his kimono?"

"I saw him from the waist down, so I don't know about his height, but his kimono was black. Perhaps it had thin stripes or a dye pattern. But to my eyes it looked plain black."

"I was with my friend looking at books," said the other student. "And I became aware of a noise, the same as him, and I saw the lattice shut, the same as him. But the man was definitely wearing a white kimono. It was a pure white kimono, no stripes or pattern."

"Isn't that odd? One of you must be mistaken."

"I certainly am not mistaken."

"Nor am I telling a lie."

I imagine that my clever readers will have probably already realized something about what these two students' mysterious statements

THE CASE OF THE MURDER ON D HILL

meant. In fact, I realized it myself. However, the people from the prosecutor's office and the police did not seem to think too deeply on this point.

Soon, the husband of the deceased, the bookseller, heard the news and came back. He was a delicate young man and did not look like a used bookseller, and when he saw his wife's corpse, his weakness was apparent and he could not speak, but tears spilled down his face. Detective Kobayashi waited for the man to settle down, then began to question him. The prosecutor also chipped in. But to their disappointment, he said that he had no idea who the culprit could be. "There is no one that holds this kind of grudge against us," he said, crying. And after making certain checks himself, he confirmed that no robber had been at work there. Thereafter, he was interrogated about his history, his wife's background, and about other matters, but there were no particular points of suspicion, and as this interrogation has no major relevance to the plot of this story I will omit it. Finally, the detective asked about the many fresh wounds on the body of the deceased. The husband was extremely hesitant, but eventually he said that he had inflicted them. However, he would not give a very clear reason for doing so, no matter how he was coaxed and questioned. But because it was known that he was out the entire evening selling at the night market, he could not be suspected of her murder even if those were marks of mistreatment. The detective must have thought so too, for he did not pry too deeply.

With that, the night's investigation was over for the time being. Our names, addresses, and so on were jotted down, Akechi's fingerprints were taken, and by the time we headed home it was already past one.

If nothing had been missed in the police's search, and it was assumed also that the witnesses were not lying, then this really was a mysterious case. And moreover, according to what I later learned, all of Detective Kobayashi's investigations that he continued to carry out from the next day onward were of no use, and not a bit of progress was made with the case after the night it happened. The witnesses were all trustworthy people. There was nothing suspicious about the residents of the eleven row houses. Inquiries were made in the victim's hometown, but there was nothing strange there either. At least, after Detective Kobayashi (the man who was widely known as a famous detective, as I said before) had searched with all his might, all he could do was conclude that the case was utterly inexplicable. Later I heard that, discouragingly, they could not find anything other than Akechi's fingerprints on the electric light switch, the only piece of evidence that Kobayashi had requested to take away. There were lots of fingerprints on the switch, but they all belonged to Akechi, perhaps because he was in a hurry at that time. The detective decided that Akechi's fingerprints had probably erased those of the culprit.

Dear readers, I wonder if reading this story you are reminded of Poe's *The Murders in the Rue Morgue* or Doyle's *The Adventure of the*

Speckled Band. In other words, I wonder if you are imagining that the culprit in this murder case is not a human but something like an orangutan or a venomous snake from India. I actually thought this myself. However, it was unthinkable that such things could be in the area of D Hill in Tokyo, and in the first place, there were witnesses who said that they had seen a man through the *shoji*. Not only that, but were it an ape or something similar, there was no way it would not have left footprints and it would have also attracted people's attention. Furthermore, the finger marks on the neck of the deceased were surely those of a human. Had a snake wound itself around her neck, it would not have left that kind of mark.

Anyway, as Akechi and I returned to our homes that evening, we spoke on many matters with great excitement. To give an example, this was the sort of thing we discussed:

"You must know of the Rose Delacourt case in Paris which became the source for Poe's *The Murder in the Rue Morgue* and Leroux's

The Mystery of the Yellow Room. Even today, over one hundred years later, there are still mysteries remaining about that strange murder case. I am reminded of it. Isn't tonight's case, with a culprit who vanishes without a trace, somewhat similar?" said Akechi.

"You're right. It really is strange. People often say that the kind of serious crime found in foreign detective novels does not happen in Japanese-style buildings, but I certainly don't think that's the case. Because this sort of incident does indeed happen. I feel that, although I don't know if I could investigate it or not, somehow I'd like to give it a shot with this case," I said.

After that we parted ways at a certain alley. I remember seeing Akechi turn down that alleyway, with his characteristic way of shaking his shoulders while he walked, and the way that his bold, block stripe *yukata* stood out in the darkness as his retreating figure quickly walked home.

The Solution

Well, one day, about ten days after the murder, I called in on Akechi Kogoro's lodgings. During those ten days, what had Akechi and I done, thought, and concluded about the case? Readers may be able to judge that sufficiently based on the conversation that was exchanged between Akechi and myself that day.

I had only seen Akechi in the café until then, and this was my first time calling upon him at his lodgings, but because I had asked him about the place before, I had no difficulty in finding it. I stood in front of a tobacconist which seemed like it might be the place and asked the lady of the shop whether Akechi was in or not.

"Yes, he's in. Please wait, I'll call for him now."

Saying this, she went to the foot of a staircase which I could see from the storefront and called loudly for Akechi. He rented the second story of this house. Then:

"Oh...."

With this strange reply, Akechi came down the creaking stairs, but upon discovering me there, he looked surprised and said, "Come right up." I followed him up to the second floor. However, when I nonchalantly took a single step into his room, I gasped in astonishment. The state of his room was just too strange. I was not unaware of the fact that Akechi was an eccentric, but this was just too eccentric.

The modest, four and a half mat—sized room was filled with books. A little of the *tatami* was visible only in the center of the room, but the rest was covered by mountains of books piled along the sliding doors and walls in each direction, their bases filling nearly the entire room and their peaks narrowing as they almost reached the ceiling, forming embankments of books on all sides. He had no other furniture. It was enough to make me wonder just how he managed to sleep in there. In the first place, there was nowhere for my host and me to sit, and any careless movement would have sent the books tumbling down at once, possibly crushing us.

"It is very cramped, and on top of that, I have no floor cushions. I'm sorry. Please find a soft-looking book to sit on top of."

I forced my way into the mountains of books and eventually found somewhere to sit. Overwhelmed, I looked around vacantly for a while.

I must venture to set out here an explanation of Akechi Kogoro, the master of this very eccentric room. Because our friendship was a recent one, I was not at all certain of many things about him—his background, how he made his living, what his goal in life was, and so on—but what was certain was that he was some sort of idler without any particular profession. At a guess I would have said he was a student, but he would have made an exceptionally strange one. He had once told me, "I am studying humanity," but at that time I did not really know what he meant. However, what I did know was that he had an extraordinary interest in crime and detectives and a fearsome wealth of knowledge.

He was about the same age as me and could not have been more than twenty-five years old. If I had to say, he was a thin man and, as I said earlier, he had a strange way of shaking his shoulders when he walked, which brought to mind Kanda Hakuryu, the professional storyteller with one disabled arm, although I do not mean to say Akechi was one of the greats, only to offer a comparison for this strange man. Speaking of Hakuryu, Akechi was his spitting image from his face to his voice. (Readers who have never seen Hakuryu should imagine, from what they know, a man who would not be called handsome, but one with the face of a genius, and a rather charming one at that.) Only, Akechi's hair was much longer and more disheveled. And he had the habit of running his fingers through his disheveled hair, often while he was talking to people, making it even more ruffled. He did not seem to care about clothing in the slightest, and he always wore a cotton kimono, cinched with a shabby-looking sash.

"Thank you so much for calling on me. I haven't seen you since then. How is the D Hill case getting on? It doesn't look like the police have much hope of catching the criminal, does it?"

Akechi ran his fingers through his hair in the way I mentioned before, while staring at my face intently.

"The truth is, I came today because I have something to discuss with you about that," I started, unsure of how to raise the subject.

"I've been thinking about a lot of things since then. Not just thinking—I've also made my own investigations at the scene, like a detective. And as a matter of fact, I've come to one conclusion. I thought that I should inform you of it...."

"Oh, that's splendid. I should like to hear all the details."

I did not miss the tinges of contempt and relief that appeared in his eyes, as if to say, "What could you know about it?" This spurred on my hesitant spirit. I steeled myself and began to talk.

"One of my friends is a newspaper reporter, and he's close to Kobayashi, the detective in charge of the case. And through this reporter I was able to learn in detail about the state of the police investigation, but it seems that their methods have gotten them nowhere. Of course, they're trying all sorts of things, but they have no particular leads. Take that electric light switch—it's useless, too. They found that the only fingerprints on it were yours. The police think it's likely that your fingerprints covered over those of the criminal. That is why, since I learned that the police are stuck, I felt that I should investigate the case even more earnestly. Now, what conclusion do you think I have reached, and why do you think I have come to speak with you before going to the police?

"Nevertheless, there's something I have

realized since the day of the incident. You must remember it too. I am speaking of the completely different accounts that the two students gave regarding the color of the suspected criminal's clothing. One said it was black, and the other said that it was white. However uncertain the human eye may be, is it not strange that they were able to mistake such opposite colors as black and white? I do not know in what way the police have interpreted it, but I believe that neither student's statement was mistaken. Do you see? The criminal was wearing clothing with black and white stripes…. In other words, a *yukata* with thick black stripes. The sort often rented out by inns…. So if you ask why it looked solid white to one person and solid black to another, this is because they saw it through the gap in the lattice of the *shoji*, and at just that second one student was in a position to see a white part of the kimono through the gap, and the other was in a position to see the black part. Although this is an unusual coincidence, it is by no means impossible. And I can think of no other way to explain the situation.

"Now, we know that the culprit wore a striped kimono, and this can be said to narrow the range of our investigation, but we still have nothing definite. The second ground for my argument is the fingerprints on the electric light switch. Using my friend, the newspaper reporter I spoke of before, I asked Detective Kobayashi to inspect those fingerprints—your fingerprints—very closely. The result confirmed beyond a doubt that I am not mistaken in my thinking. By the way, would you be so good as to loan me an inkstone for a moment, if you have one?"

Then, I tried an experiment. First borrowing the inkstone, I put a thin layer of ink on my right thumb and pressed a single fingerprint on a piece of writing paper from my pocket. Next, I waited for the fingerprint to dry, then put ink on the same finger again and carefully pressed it down again over the first print, this time changing my finger's direction. When I did this, the tangled double layers of both fingerprints were clearly visible.

"The police's explanation is that your fingerprints were on top of the culprit's and erased them, but as we can see from this experiment now that is impossible. No matter how hard you press down, fingerprints are made up of lines, and between the lines there should still be traces of the previous fingerprints. If the previous fingerprints were exactly the same as the new ones and their placement also did not differ at all, then each line of the fingerprints would match, or the new fingerprints might also cover the previous ones, but such a thing is unbelievable first of all, and even if it were true it would not change my conclusion in this case.

"However, if the culprit was the one who turned off the light, he must have left his fingerprints on the switch. I wondered if the police might have overlooked the earlier fingerprints that remained between the lines of your fingerprints, and I tried examining it myself, but there was not the slightest trace. In short, the only fingerprints on that switch, both before and after, were yours. As for why there were no fingerprints from the people at the secondhand bookstore, I do not know, but perhaps the light in that room was always left on, and had never been turned off.

"So what does this all mean? My thinking goes like this. A man wearing a kimono with rough stripes, a man who could be the childhood friend of the dead woman and may have been motivated by this lost love, knew that the owner of the secondhand bookstore went out to sell at night markets and this man attacked the woman while he was out. She must have known this man well, because there is no evidence that she cried out or struggled. Then, having thoroughly completed his objective, the man turned off the electric light in order to delay the discovery of the corpse and walked away. However, the man's one mistake was that he didn't know that the lattice of the *shoji* was open, and that when he shut it in surprise, he was seen by two students who were in the storefront by chance. Then, once the man was outside, he suddenly realized that when he turned off the electric light he must have left fingerprints on the switch. These had to be erased no matter what. But it would be dangerous for him to sneak into the room again in the same way. But then a bright idea came to him. This idea was to be the one to discover the murder himself. By doing so, not only would he simply be able to eliminate himself from suspicion regarding the earlier fingerprints by turning on the light himself without seeming the slightest bit unnatural, but who would ever think that the person who discovered the crime would be the culprit himself? So it was doubly to his benefit, you see. In this way, he watched the police's methods with the appearance of innocence. In his audacity he even gave a statement. And the result was a bull's-eye, just as he imagined. Five, ten days on, still no one has come to arrest him."

With what expression did Akechi Kogoro listen to my story? I expected that he would make some sort of strange expression or cut me off as I spoke. But to my surprise, his face appeared expressionless. Although he was not ordinarily the kind to let his feelings show, he was far too calm. He had sat silently ruffling his hair from start to finish. Wondering just how shameless a man he could be, I proceeded to my final point.

"You are going to ask me, if that's true, then where did the culprit enter and how did he flee? Certainly, if that point cannot be clarified then knowing all the rest is to no avail. But unfortunately for you I've found this out as well. The result of the investigation that evening appeared to be that there was absolutely no trace of the culprit leaving. But seeing as there was a murder, there is no way that the culprit did not come and go somehow, so I could only think that something had been overlooked in the detectives' search. Although the police had taken considerable pains, unfortunately, they were no match for a mere student: me.

"Well, actually, it was a simple matter, you see. This is what I thought: first, the police had already questioned everyone thoroughly, so there was no reason to doubt the people of the neighborhood. That being the case, might the culprit not have taken his leave in a way that, even if he caught someone's attention, they would not realized that he was the culprit? Then if someone had witnessed him leaving, it would not be a problem, right? In other words, he might have made use of a blind spot in people's attentiveness—yes, just as there are blind spots in our vision, there are blind spots in our powers of attention, too—and hidden himself, just as a magician somehow hides a large object before the very eyes of his viewers. Then, I set my eyes on Asahiya, the *soba* store two doors down from the secondhand bookstore."

The watchmaker and the confectioner's stood to the right of the bookstore, and to the left stood a *tabi* store and the *soba* store.

"I went there and asked them if a man had asked to use the facilities at around eight o'clock on the night of the incident. I am sure you are familiar with Asahiya yourself, but the dirt floor there extends from the shop to a back door, and the facilities are just outside the back door, so if one uses the lavatory there, they must go out the back door and come back in again. Because the ice cream man has his store at the corner where the alley comes out, there is no way he would see. And because it is a *soba* restaurant, it is the most natural thing to ask to use the lavatory. Upon asking, I heard that on that evening the lady of the house was out and only the owner was in the store, making it ideal. What a splendid idea, don't you think?

"Sure enough, there was a customer who had used the lavatory at precisely the hour and minute in question. But, unfortunately, the owner of Asahiya could not remember the man's face or whether he was wearing a striped kimono. I immediately passed this on to Detective Kobayashi through my friend. The detective went and investigated the *soba* place himself, but he found out nothing further."

I paused slightly to give Akechi room to respond. In this position, he could not possibly fail to say something this time. However, he just kept running his fingers through his hair as always while looking on with an air of superiority. Until this point I had been using indirect methods out of respect for him, but now I had to change to more direct methods.

"Look, Akechi, you know what I'm getting at here. Irrefutable evidence is pointing at you. I confess, from the bottom of my heart, that I somehow cannot bring myself to doubt you, but when all the evidence is put together like this, I don't see what other solution there is.... I wondered if one of the people in those row houses had a *yukata* with bold stripes, and I took great pains to investigate, but no one did. That is believable. Even if someone did have the same striped *yukata*, it's rare to wear clothes that flashy. Besides, the trick with the fingerprints and the trick with using the conveniences were really clever—these are tricks that could not be imitated in the slightest by someone who wasn't a crime scholar like yourself. And then, the strangest thing was, although you've said that the deceased was a childhood friend of yours, that night, when they were looking into the wife's background, you were listening and you did not state this at all, did you?

"Now, the only thing you have left to rely upon is whether or not you have an alibi. But that is useless too. Do you remember, on our way home that night, how I asked you where you had been before coming to the White Plum Blossom Café? You answered that you had been strolling around the area for about an hour. If someone had seen you out for a walk, it would've been a natural thing to stop during your walk and use the conveniences at the *soba* place, wouldn't it? Is what I've said mistaken, Akechi? How about it? If possible may I hear your explanation?"

Dear readers, what do you think that odd fellow Akechi Kogoro did when I finished speaking? Do you think he may have prostrated himself in shame? Why on earth I do not know, but I was taken aback by his completely unexpected reaction. Which is to say, he suddenly guffawed.

"Oh, how rude of me, how rude. I certainly do not mean to laugh at you, but you just looked so serious," Akechi said by way of defense. "Your ideas are quite interesting. I am delighted to have found a friend like you. But regrettably, your reasoning is a bit superficial and materialist. Take this for an example. As concerns my relationship with that woman, did you attempt a probing, psychological investigation into what sort of childhood friends we were? Or into whether I had a romantic relationship with that woman previously? Or indeed whether I held a grudge against her? Couldn't you even figure those things out? As for why I did not say on that night that I knew her, the reason is simple. I did not know anything which would be useful as reference. We had already parted ways before we had even entered elementary school. Although recently, by chance, I had learned it was her and we had spoken two or three times."

"Then what, for instance, should one think

about the fingerprints?"

"Do you think I have done nothing since that evening? I have done quite a bit with the case myself. I wander around D Hill nearly every day. In particular I went to the secondhand bookstore quite a lot. I cornered the proprietor and probed into all sorts of matters. I confided in him then that I had known his wife, but that was actually to my advantage. Just as you learned of the state of the police investigation through a reporter, I got information about it from the proprietor of the secondhand bookstore. I also soon learned about the fingerprints of which you speak, and thinking it was strange myself I made some investigations, but, ha ha.... It's a funny story. The wires in the light bulb had disconnected. Nobody turned it off at all. It was my mistake to think that the light came on because I twisted the switch; when I did so, in my panic I jostled the light, and so the previously disconnected tungsten reconnected then. It is perfectly natural, then, that only my fingerprints were found on the switch. You told me that evening that you had seen the light on through the gaps in the *shoji*. If that is so, then the light bulb must have gotten disconnected after that. Those old light bulbs do sometimes break on their own, without anyone doing anything, you know. Now, then, as for the color of the culprit's kimono, rather than explain that myself...."

Saying that, he began to dig here and there in the mountains of books that surrounded him, until eventually he dug out one old, worn Western book.

"Have you ever read this? It's a book called *On the Witness Stand* by Munsterberg. Please take a look at just these ten lines at the beginning of this chapter called 'Illusions.'"

As I listened to his confident reasoning, I became gradually aware of my own failure. I took the book from him and read, just as I had been told. What was written there was roughly as follows.

There had been an automobile accident. Before the court, one of the witnesses who had sworn to tell "the whole truth, and nothing but the truth," declared that the entire road was dry and dusty; the other swore that it had rained and the road was muddy. The one said that the automobile was running very slowly; the other, that he had never seen an automobile rushing more rapidly. The first swore that there were only two or three people on the village road; the other, that a large number of men, women, and children were passing by. Both witnesses were highly respectable gentlemen, neither of whom had the slightest interest in changing the facts as he remembered them.

Akechi waited for me to finish reading this, and then as he turned the pages again he spoke.

"That was something which actually occurred. Now, there's this chapter called

'The Memory of the Witness.' Nearly halfway through there is a story of an experiment which was planned in advance. It does involve the color of clothing, so please give it a read although it may be bothersome to do so."

It was the following account.

[...] There was, for instance, two years ago [the book was published in 1911] in Göttingen a meeting of a scientific association, made up of jurists, psychologists, and physicians, all, therefore, men well trained in careful observation. Somewhere in the same street there was that evening a public festivity of the carnival. Suddenly, in the midst of the scholarly meeting, the doors open, a clown in highly colored costume rushes in in mad excitement, and a Negro with a revolver in hand follows him. In the middle of the hall first the one, then the other, shouts wild phrases; then the one falls to the ground, the other jumps on him; then a shot, and suddenly both are out of the room. The whole affair took less than twenty seconds. All were completely taken by surprise, and no one, with the exception of the President, had the slightest idea that every word and action had been rehearsed beforehand, or that photographs had been taken of the scene. It seemed most natural that the President should beg the members to write down individually an exact report, inasmuch as he felt sure that the matter would come before the courts. *(I have omitted a passage here reporting that their memories were full of mistakes and giving percentages.)* Only four persons, for instance, among forty noticed that the Negro had nothing on his head; the others gave him a derby, or a high hat, and so on. In addition to this, a red suit, a brown one, a striped one, a coffee-colored jacket, shirt sleeves, and similar costumes were invented for him. He wore in reality white trousers and a black jacket with a large red necktie. [...]

"As Munsterberg shrewdly observed," Akechi began, "people's observations and memories are not to be relied upon. Even the scholars in this example were not able to tell apart the colors of his clothing. Do I think it is impossible that those students mistook the kimono's color that night? They may have seen someone. But that person was not wearing a striped kimono. Of course, it was not me. The observation you hit upon about the striped *yukata* seen through the gaps in the lattice is rather interesting in and of itself, but is it not a little too perfect? Could you not at least believe in my innocence rather than such a concurrence of coincidences? Then, finally, we come to the man who asked to use the *soba* seller's lavatory. On this point I had the same idea as you. Try as I might, I thought of no other route for the culprit to take but through Asahiya. So I also went there and investigated, but the result was, unfortunately, that I reached the opposite conclusion from you. In fact, there was no man who used the lavatory."

As the reader has likely already noticed,

Akechi had thus repudiated the testimony of the witnesses, the culprit's fingerprints, and even the culprit's passageway in an attempt to prove his own innocence, but at the same time, was he not repudiating the crime itself? I did not have the slightest idea what he was thinking.

"Then, you have an idea of who the culprit is?"

"I do," he answered, ruffling his hair. "My approach is a little different from yours. Physical evidence and so on all depends on how you interpret it. The best method of detection is to see into the human mind psychologically. But this is a matter of the detective's own ability. Anyway, I tried to put the emphasis in that direction this time.

"The first thing that attracted my attention was the fact that there were fresh wounds on the body of the bookseller's wife. Shortly thereafter, I heard that there were similar wounds on the body of the *soba* man's wife.

I'm sure you know this as well. However, these women's husbands did not seem like that sort of violent man. Both the bookseller and the *soba* man are unassuming, sensible men, as you know. Somehow, I could not help but suspect there was some secret concealed there. So first I collared the bookseller to try to get the secret out from his own lips. Because I said that I had been an acquaintance of his dead wife, this put him somewhat at ease and it went relatively easily. Then, I was able to get a certain strange fact out of him. However, next was the proprietor of the *soba* place, and he is, despite appearances, a rather strong-headed man, so it required some hard work to get anything out of him. But by means of a certain process I was highly successful.

"I'm sure you know that the psychological associative approach to diagnosis has begun to be used in criminal investigations as well. It is a method by which lots of simple trigger words are given and the speed at which the suspect forms associations is measured. However, I am not necessarily limited to saying simple trigger words such as 'dog,' 'house,' or 'river,' as psychologists are, nor do I believe there is always a need for the help of a chronoscope. For one who has the knack of it, such formalities are not especially needed. As proof of that, didn't the people of old who were called great judges or detectives unknowingly practice these psychological methods using only their natural talents, long before psychology had developed to the state it is in today? Ooka, the Governor of Echizen, was certainly one such person. Or to speak of novels, there is a part at the beginning of Poe's *The Murders in the Rue Morgue* where Dupin correctly guesses what is on his friend's mind from one single movement of his body, does he not? Doyle mimics this—in *The Adventure of the Resident Patient*, Holmes makes his usual reasoning, but they are all associative diagnoses of a sort. The variety of mechanical methods of psychologists are simply made for ordinary men without these gifts of insight. I have digressed slightly, but in this sense, I used associative techniques of a sort with the *soba* man. I devised a number of traps for him in our conversation, and a very dull chat it was, too. And then I studied his psychological reaction. But as this was an extremely delicate psychological problem, as well as a rather complex one, I shall save the details for when we speak at leisure. At any rate, as a result I reached a conclusion. In other words, I found the culprit.

"However, I don't have a single piece of physical evidence. Therefore I cannot take it to the police. Even if I went to them, I doubt they would listen. Besides, I have another reason for folding my arms and watching, despite knowing who the culprit is, and that is because the criminal did not have the slightest bit of malice. It is a strange way to put it, but this murder was carried out on the agreement of the culprit and the victim. No, perhaps you could say it was carried out according to the victim's wishes."

I turned various ideas over in my mind, but I was unable to understand what he was thinking at all. I forgot to be ashamed of my own failure and bent my ear to listen to his fantastic reasoning.

"So, if I may tell you my idea, the murderer is the proprietor of Asahiya. He told the story about the man using the lavatory in order to hide his crime. But no, that was not his invention in the least. We are the ones to blame. Both you and I asked him whether there had been such a man, and this was like instigating him. On top of this, he must have mistaken us for detectives or the like. Now, as for why he committed the murder.... I feel that this case has allowed me to see some of the most surprising and pathetic secrets that are hidden behind the façade of this world, which is seemingly so very innocent. This is, indeed, the type of thing which can only be found in the world of nightmares.

"The proprietor of Asahiya has followed in the footsteps of the Marquis de Sade and is a terrible sadist, and what a twist of fate to discover two doors down a woman Masoch. The bookseller's wife was equal to him in her masochism. So, with the cleverness specific to their particular sickness, they committed adultery without being found out by anyone....

The Case of the Murder on D Hill

You see now what I meant by this being a murder by consent.... Until recently the abnormal desires of each had just barely been met by their legitimate spouse. That the bookseller's wife and the man from Asahiya's wife had the same sort of wounds is proof of that. But it need hardly be said that this did not satisfy them. So when they found the person they had each been searching for right under their nose, it is not difficult to imagine that they came to a very quick understanding with each other, is it? But the result was more than a trick of fate. Due to their synthesis of passive and active forces, their disgraceful behavior started building in intensity. And finally, on that night, it was the cause of an incident they certainly never had hoped for...."

I shuddered involuntarily as I heard Akechi's bizarre conclusion. What a strange case this one was!

Just then, the mistress of the tobacconist downstairs brought up the evening paper. Akechi accepted it and took a look at the local news page, and before long, he sighed gently.

"Oh, it looks like he couldn't take it anymore and gave himself up. What a strange coincidence, to receive news like this just when we were talking about it."

I looked at where he was pointing. There, with a small headline and just ten lines of text, it was noted that the proprietor of Asahiya had turned himself in.

Word List

- 本文で使われている全ての語を掲載しています（LEVEL 1、2）。ただし、LEVEL 3以上は、中学校レベルの語を含みません。
- 語形が規則変化する語の見出しは原形で示しています。不規則変化語は本文中で使われている形になっています。
- 一般的な意味を紹介していますので、一部の語で本文で実際に使われている品詞や意味と合っていないことがあります。
- 品詞は以下のように示しています。

名 名詞	代 代名詞	形 形容詞	副 副詞	動 動詞	助 助動詞
前 前置詞	接 接続詞	間 間投詞	冠 冠詞	略 略語	俗 俗語
頭 接頭語	尾 接尾語	記 記号	関 関係代名詞		

A

- ☐ **a ~ or two** 1~か2~、2, 3の
- ☐ **aback** 熟 taken aback 驚く、びっくりさせられる、困惑する
- ☐ **abandon** 動 諦める、断念する
- ☐ **aberrant** 形 常軌を逸した、異常な
- ☐ **ability** 名 ①できること、(~する)能力 ②才能
- ☐ **abnormal** 形 異常な、正常でない
- ☐ **about** 熟 be about to まさに~しようとしている、~するところである care about ~を気に掛ける How about ~? ~はどうですか。~しませんか。 run about 走り回る
- ☐ **abroad** 熟 from abroad 海外から
- ☐ **abruptly** 副 不意に、突然、急に
- ☐ **absentmindedly** 副 上の空で、ぼんやりと
- ☐ **absolutely** 副 完全に、確実に
- ☐ **absorb** 動 吸収する be absorbed in ~に没頭して
- ☐ **accept** 動 ①受け入れる ②同意する、認める
- ☐ **accident** 名 (不慮の)事故、災難
- ☐ **accompany** 動 ①ついていく、つきそう ②(~に)ともなって起こる
- ☐ **accomplish** 動 成し遂げる、果たす
- ☐ **accord** 名 調和、一致
- ☐ **according** 副《- to ~》~によれば[よると]
- ☐ **account** 名 ①計算書 ②勘定、預金口座 ③説明、報告、記述
- ☐ **acquaintance** 名 ①知人、知り合い ②面識、知識
- ☐ **acquire** 動 ①(努力して)獲得する、確保する ②(学力、技術などを)習得する
- ☐ **act** 動 ①行動する ②機能する ③演じる
- ☐ **active** 形 ①活動的な ②積極的な ③活動[作動]中の
- ☐ **activity** 名 活動、活気
- ☐ **actually** 副 実際に、本当に、実は
- ☐ **add** 動 ①加える、足す ②足し算をする ③言い添える
- ☐ **addition** 名 ①付加、追加、添加 ②足し算 in addition 加えて、さらに
- ☐ **additionally** 副 その上、さらに
- ☐ **address** 名 ①住所、アドレス ②演説 動 ①あて名を書く ②演説をする、話しかける
- ☐ **adequate** 形 十分な、ふさわしい、

Word List

適切な
- **adjust** 動 調整する
- **adjustment** 名 ①調整, 調節 ②適応
- **admirer** 名 崇拝者, 賛美者, ファン
- **admit** 動 認める, 許可する, 入れる
- **adore** 動 崇拝する, あこがれる
- **adultery** 名 不倫, 不貞
- **advance** 名 進歩, 前進 **in advance** 前もって, あらかじめ
- **advantage** 名 有利な点[立場], 強み, 優越
- **adventure** 名 冒険
- **Adventure of the Resident Patient** 『入院患者』《アーサー・コナン・ドイルによる短編小説》
- **Adventure of the Speckled Band** 『まだらの紐』《アーサー・コナン・ドイルによる短編小説》
- **affair** 名 事柄, 事件
- **affection** 名 愛情, 感情
- **aforementioned** 形 前述[上記]の
- **after a while** しばらくして
- **after all** やはり, 結局
- **afterward** 副 その後, のちに
- **agreement** 名 ①合意, 協定 ②一致
- **ah** 間 《驚き・悲しみ・賞賛などを表して》ああ, やっぱり
- **aimless** 形 目的のない, あてのない
- **Akechi Kogoro** 明智小五郎《人名》
- **alert** 動 警報を出す, 警戒させる
- **alibi** 名 アリバイ, 現場不在証明
- **all** 熟 **after all** やはり, 結局 **all day** 一日中, 明けても暮れても **all kinds of** さまざまな, あらゆる種類の **all over** 全体に亘って **at all** とにかく **first of all** まず第一に **not at all** 少しも~でない **not ~ at all** 少しも[全然]~ない
- **alley** 名 路地, 裏通り, 小道
- **alleyway** 名 (狭い)裏通り
- **allow** 動 ①許す, 《- … to ~》…が~するのを可能にする, …に~させておく ②与える
- **allure** 名 魅力, 魅惑
- **along with** ~と一緒に
- **alpaca** 名 アルパカ毛[生地・毛製品]
- **although** 接 ~だけれども, ~にもかかわらず, たとえ~でも
- **always** 熟 **as always** いつものように
- **amazing** 形 驚くべき, 見事な
- **ambassador** 名 大使, 使節
- **amongst** 前 の間に[を・で]
- **amount** 動 (総計~に)なる
- **amuse** 動 楽しませる
- **amusement** 名 娯楽, 楽しみ
- **anew** 副 新たに, 再び
- **angle** 名 ①角度 ②角
- **another** 熟 **one another** お互い **yet another** さらにもう一つの
- **anxiety** 名 ①心配, 不安 ②切望
- **anxious** 形 ①心配な, 不安な ②切望して
- **anymore** 副 《通例否定文, 疑問文で》今はもう, これ以上, これから
- **anyone** 代 ①《疑問文・条件節で》誰か ②《否定文で》誰も (~ない) ③《肯定文で》誰でも **for anyone who do** ~する全てに人にとって
- **anything else** ほかの何か
- **anyway** 副 ①いずれにせよ, ともかく ②どんな方法でも
- **apart** 副 ①ばらばらに, 離れて ②別にして, それだけで **tell apart** 見分ける
- **ape** 名 サル, 類人猿

- □ **apology** 名 謝罪, 釈明
- □ **appalling** 形 恐ろしい, ぞっとさせる
- □ **apparent** 形 明らかな, 明白な, 見かけの, 外見上の
- □ **appeal** 動 ①求める, 訴える ②(人の)気に入る 名 ①要求, 訴え ②魅力, 人気
- □ **appear** 動 ①現れる, 見えてくる ②(~のように)見える, ~らしい　appear to するように見える
- □ **appearance** 名 ①現れること, 出現 ②外見, 印象
- □ **appetite** 名 ①食欲 ②欲求
- □ **apprentice** 名 見習い, 徒弟
- □ **approach** 動 ①接近する ②話を持ちかける 名 接近, (~へ)近づく道
- □ **ardent** 形 熱心な, 熱烈な
- □ **argument** 名 ①議論, 論争 ②論拠, 理由
- □ **armchair** 名 ひじ掛けいす, ひじ置き
- □ **armpit** 名 腋の下のくぼみ, 腋窩
- □ **armrest** 名 アームレスト, 肘掛け
- □ **army** 名 軍隊, 《the –》陸軍
- □ **arrangement** 名 ①準備, 手配 ②取り決め, 協定 ③整理, 配置
- □ **arrest** 動 逮捕する
- □ **arrival** 名 ①到着 ②到達
- □ **arrogant** 形 尊大な, 傲慢な, 無礼な, 横柄な
- □ **art** 熟 work of art ~の仕事
- □ **article** 名 (新聞・雑誌などの)記事, 論文
- □ **artisan** 名 伝統工芸などの職人, 熟練工
- □ **artist** 名 芸術家
- □ **artistic** 形 芸術的な, 芸術(家)の
- □ **as** 熟 as a matter of fact 実際は, 実のところ　as a result その結果(として)　as a result of ~の結果(とし

て)　as always いつものように　as ~ as one can できる限り~　as for ~に関しては, ~はどうかと言うと　as if あたかも~のように, まるで~みたいに　as much as ~と同じだけ　as per ~のとおり　as soon as ~するとすぐ, ~するや否や　as though あたかも~のように, まるで~みたいに　as to ~に関しては, ~については, ~に応じて　as usual いつものように, 相変わらず　as well なお, その上, 同様に　as well as ~と同様に　as you know ご存知のとおり　be known as ~として知られている　just as (ちょうど)であろうとおり　not so much as ~ほどではない　not so ~ as … …ほど~でない　so ~ as to … …するほど~で　such as たとえば~, ~のような　such ~ as … …のような　the same ~ as … …と同じ(ような)~　times as … as … AA の~倍の…

- □ **Asahiya** 名 旭屋《蕎麦屋の名》
- □ **ashamed** 形 恥じた, 気が引けた, 《be – of ~》~が恥ずかしい, ~を恥じている
- □ **aside** 副 わきへ(に), 離れて
- □ **ask ~ if** ~かどうか尋ねる
- □ **aspiration** 名 ①熱望, 願望, 抱負 ②呼吸
- □ **association** 名 ①交際, 連合, 結合 ②連想 ③協会, 組合
- □ **associative** 形 連想の
- □ **assume** 動 ①仮定する, 当然のことと思う ②引き受ける
- □ **astonishing** 形 驚くべき
- □ **astonishment** 名 驚き
- □ **attach** 動 ①取り付ける, 添える ②付随する, 帰属する
- □ **attachment** 名 ①愛着 ②取り付け, 付属品, 添付
- □ **attack** 動 襲う, 攻める
- □ **attempt** 動 試みる, 企てる 名 試み, 企て, 努力

Word List

- **attention** 图①注意, 集中 ②配慮, 手当て, 世話 **pay attention** 注意[留意・注目]する
- **attentiveness** 图注意力
- **attract** 動①引きつける, 引く ②魅力がある, 魅了する
- **attractive** 形魅力的な, あいきょうのある
- **attribute** 图特性, 属性
- **auction** 图競売, オークション
- **audacity** 图大胆さ, 厚かましさ
- **author** 图著者, 作家
- **automatically** 副無意識に, 自動的に, 惰性的に
- **automobile** 图自動車
- **avail** 图効力, 益 **to no avail**(努力などが)無駄に
- **average** 图平均(値), 並み 形平均の, 普通の
- **avoid** 動避ける, (~を)しないようにする
- **aware** 形①気がついて, 知って ②(~の)認識のある
- **awful** 形①ひどい, 不愉快な ②恐ろしい
- **awkwardness** 图ぎこちなさ, 気まずさ

B

- **background** 图背景, 前歴, 生い立ち
- **backrest** 图背もたれ
- **band** 图ひも, 帯
- **bare** 形裸の, むき出しの
- **barely** 副①かろうじて, やっと ②ほぼ, もう少しで
- **base** 图基礎, 土台, 本部 動《 – on ~》~に基礎を置く, 基づく
- **basic** 形基礎の, 基本の
- **basis** 图①土台, 基礎 ②基準, 原理 ③根拠
- **bathhouse** 图風呂屋
- **bathing** 图水浴び, 海水浴, 水泳
- **bathroom** 图手洗い, トイレ
- **bear** 動①運ぶ ②支える ③耐える
- **beaten** 動 beat (打つ)の過去分詞 形打たれた, 打ち負かされた, 疲れ切った
- **beauty** 图①美, 美しい人[物]
- **because of** ~のために, ~の理由で
- **bedroom** 图寝室
- **before long** やがて, まもなく
- **beforehand** 副①あらかじめ, 前もって ②早まって
- **beg** 動懇願する, お願いする
- **beginning** 图初め, 始まり
- **behave** 動振る舞う
- **behavior** 图振る舞い, 態度, 行動
- **behind** 前①~の後ろに, ~の背後に ②~に遅れて, ~に劣って 副①後ろに, 背後に ②遅れて, 劣って **leave behind** あとにする, ~を置き去りにする
- **being** 動 be (~である)の現在分詞 **for the time being** 今のところは 图存在, 生命, 人間 **human being** 人, 人間
- **believable** 形信じられる, 真実味のある
- **believe in** ~を信じる
- **bellboy** 图(ホテルなどの)ボーイ
- **belong to** ~に属する
- **beloved** 图最愛の人
- **bench** 图ベンチ, 長いす
- **bend** 動①曲がる, 曲げる ②屈服する[させる]
- **beneath** 前~の下に[の], ~より低い
- **benefit** 图利益, 恩恵

Short Stories by Edogawa Ranpo

- □ **bent** 動 bend（曲がる）の過去, 過去分詞
- □ **besides** 副 その上, さらに
- □ **best** 熟 do one's best 全力を尽くす
- □ **bet** 名 賭け, 掛け金（の対象）
- □ **better off dead** 死んだほうがましだ
- □ **beyond** 前 ～を越えて, ～の向こうに
- □ **bit** 名 ①小片, 少量 ②《a－》少し, ちょっと
- □ **bizarre** 形 奇妙な, 奇抜な, 異様な
- □ **blade** 名 ①（刀・ナイフなどの）刃 ②（麦・稲などの）葉 ③（オールの）水かき, ブレード shoulder blade 肩甲骨
- □ **blame** 動 とがめる, 非難する
- □ **bleed** 動 出血する, 血を流す[流させる]
- □ **blind spot** （見落しがちな）盲点
- □ **block stripe** 棒縞
- □ **blood** 名 血, 血液
- □ **bloom** 動 咲く, 咲かせる
- □ **blossom** 名 花
- □ **boarding house** 下宿(屋)
- □ **bodily** 形 身体上の, 体の
- □ **bold** 形 際立った,（線など）肉太の
- □ **boldfaced** 形 面の皮の厚い, ずうずうしい
- □ **bone** 名 骨,《-s》骨格
- □ **bookseller** 名 本屋, 書籍商
- □ **bookshelf** 名 本棚
- □ **bookstore** 名 書店
- □ **boot** 熟 to boot おまけに, その上
- □ **born into** 《be－》～に生まれる
- □ **bosom** 名 （特に女性の）胸
- □ **bothersome** 形 煩わしい, 面倒くさい
- □ **bottom** 名 底, 下部, すそ野, ふもと, 最下位, 根底
- □ **bounce** 動 ①弾む, 跳ね上がる ②弾ませる, 跳ね返す
- □ **bound** 名 境界(線), 限界
- □ **break into** ～に押し入る, 急に～する
- □ **breath** 名 息, 呼吸 out of breath 息を切らして
- □ **breathe** 動 呼吸する
- □ **breathing** 名 呼吸, 息づかい
- □ **brief** 形 短い時間の
- □ **bring up** 上に持ってくる
- □ **broad** 形 幅の広い
- □ **broad-striped** 形 棒縞の
- □ **brouhaha** 名 騒動, 大騒ぎ
- □ **bruise** 動 （人や果物に）傷をつける 名 打撲傷
- □ **brutally** 副 残忍に, 残酷に
- □ **bubble** 動 泡立つ, 沸き立つ
- □ **building** 名 建物, 建造物, ビルディング
- □ **bulb** 名 ①電球 ②バルブ ③球根 light bulb 電球
- □ **bulbous** 形 ふくらんだ
- □ **bulky** 形 大きい, かさばる
- □ **bull's-eye** 的中, 大当たり
- □ **bundle** 名 束, 包み, 一巻き
- □ **burly** 形 がっしりした, たくましい
- □ **burn with** ～を強く感じる
- □ **burst** 動 ①爆発する[させる] ②破裂する[させる] burst into 急に～する
- □ **buttock** 名 《通例-s》尻
- □ **buyer** 名 買い手, バイヤー

C

- □ **café** 名 カフェ, 喫茶店
- □ **call for** ～を呼び求める, 呼び出す

Word List

- **call in** ~を呼ぶ, ~に立ち寄る
- **call on** 呼びかける, 招集する, 求める, 訪問する
- **call out** 叫ぶ, 呼び出す, 声を掛ける
- **call upon** 求める, 頼む, 訪問する
- **calm** 形 穏やかな, 落ち着いた
- **camp** 動 野営する, キャンプする camp out 長居する
- **can** 熟 as ~ as one can できる限り~
- **cannot help ~ing** ~せずにはいられない
- **capable** 形 ①《be – of ~ [~ing]》~の能力 [資質] がある ②有能な
- **care** 熟 care about ~を気に掛ける take care 気をつける, 注意する
- **careless** 形 不注意な, うかつな
- **caress** 名 愛撫, 抱擁
- **carnival** 名 カーニバル, 謝肉祭
- **carpet** 名 じゅうたん, 敷物
- **carry out** 外へ運び出す, [計画を] 実行する
- **cart** 名 荷馬車, 荷車 動 運ぶ cart off 運び去る
- **carve** 動 彫刻する
- **cast** 動 投げる cast one's eye over ~に目を向ける
- **catalogue** 名 目録, カタログ
- **cavity** 名 空洞
- **ceiling** 名 天井
- **celebrated** 形 名高い, 有名な
- **central** 形 中央の, 主要な
- **certain** 形 ①確実な, 必ず~する ②(人が) 確信した ③ある ④いくらかの
- **certainly** 副 確かに, 必ず
- **challenging** 形 能力が試される, やる気をそそる
- **chance** 熟 by chance 偶然, たまたま
- **chandelier** 名 シャンデリア
- **chapter** 名 (書物の) 章
- **character** 名 ①特性, 個性 ②(小説・劇などの) 登場人物 ③品性, 人格
- **characteristic** 形 特徴のある, 独特の
- **charge** 名 ①請求金額, 料金 ②責任 ③非難, 告発 face charges for ~で告訴される in charge of ~を任されて, ~を担当して, ~の責任を負って
- **charm** 名 魅力, 魔力
- **charming** 形 魅力的な, チャーミングな
- **chat** 動 おしゃべりをする, 談笑する
- **check** 名 照合, 検査
- **cheerful** 形 上機嫌の, 元気のよい, (人を) 気持ちよくさせる
- **cheery** 形 元気いっぱいの, 陽気な
- **chest** 名 胸
- **chief** 名 頭, 長, 親分 形 最高位の, 第一の, 主要な chief inspector 警察署の司法主任
- **childhood** 名 幼年 [子ども] 時代
- **chip in** 口を出す, 人の話に割り込む
- **chisel** 名 のみ, たがね, 彫刻刀
- **choice** 名 選択 (の範囲・自由), えり好み, 選択した人 [物] have no choice but to ~するしかない
- **chronoscope** 名 クロノスコープ, 弾速計
- **chrysanthemum** 名 キク (菊) chrysanthemum doll 菊人形
- **churn** 動 ①かくはんする, 激しくかき回す ②激しく動く churn out 大量生産する, 量産する
- **chuugata** 名 中形《中ぐらいの大きさの型紙を使った染め模様。また, その模様の浴衣地》

113

- **cigar** 名 葉巻
- **cigarette** 名 (紙巻)たばこ
- **cinch** 動 ~をしっかり締める
- **circle** 名 ①円, 円周, 輪 ②循環, 軌道 ③仲間, サークル
- **circumstance** 名 ①(周囲の)事情, 状況, 環境 ②《-s》(人の)境遇, 生活状態
- **civil** 形 ①一般人の, 民間(人)の ②国内の, 国家の ③礼儀正しい **civil servant** 公務員
- **clap** 動 (手を)たたく
- **clarify** 動 ①明確にする, 解明する ②浄化する
- **clear** 形 ①はっきりした, 明白な ②澄んだ ③(よく)晴れた
- **clearly** 副 明らかに, はっきりと
- **clerk** 名 事務員, 店員
- **clever** 形 ①頭のよい, 利口な ②器用な, 上手な
- **cleverness** 名 賢さ, 利口さ
- **client** 名 依頼人, 顧客, クライアント
- **climb into** ~に乗り込む
- **cloak** 名 マント, 袖なし外とう
- **clomp** 動 ドシンドシンと歩く
- **close to** ①《be-》~に近い ②《get-》~に近づく, 接近する
- **closely** 副 ①密接に ②念入りに, 詳しく ③ぴったりと
- **clothing** 名 衣類, 衣料品
- **clown** 名 道化(役者), おどけ者
- **clue** 名 手がかり, 糸口
- **clumsy** 形 ぎこちない, 不器用な
- **coax** 動 (人)をうまく説得する, (人)をおだてる, ~を引き[聞き]出す
- **coffee-colored** 形 暗褐色の
- **coincidence** 名 同時発生, 一致, 合致
- **collar** 動 (人を)引きとめる
- **colored** 形 色のついた
- **colorful** 形 カラフルな, 派手な
- **come** 熟 **come back** 戻る **come down** 下りて来る **come in** 中にいる, やってくる **come on** スイッチが入る **come out** 出てくる, 出掛ける, 姿を現す **come out of** ~から出てくる, ~をうまく乗り越える **come running** 飛んでくる, かけつける **come to think of it** 考えてみると **come up with** ~に追いつく, ~を思いつく, 考え出す, 見つけ出す
- **comfort** 名 ①快適さ, 満足 ②慰め ③安楽
- **comfortable** 形 快適な, 心地いい
- **commit** 動 ①委託する ②引き受ける ③(罪などを)犯す **commit a crime** 罪を犯す
- **commotion** 名 ①激動 ②騒動, 騒ぎ
- **company** 熟 **in someone's company** (人)と一緒に
- **compare** 動 ①比較する, 対照する ②たとえる
- **comparison** 名 比較, 対照
- **compel** 動 (人に)強制する, しいる, ~させる
- **complete** 形 完全な, まったくの, 完成した **complete and utter** まったくの
- **completely** 副 完全に, すっかり
- **completion** 名 完成, 完結
- **complex** 形 入り組んだ, 複雑な, 複合の
- **complicate** 形 複雑な, 込み入った
- **compose** 動 作曲する, (詩などを)書く
- **comprise** 動 ①(~より)成る ②包含する
- **conceal** 動 隠す, 秘密にする
- **concern** 名 ①関心事 ②関心, 心配 ③関係, 重要性 **going concern**

WORD LIST

継続企業
- **conclude** 動 ①終える, 完結する ②結論を下す
- **conclusion** 名 結論, 結末
- **concurrence** 名 一致, 符合
- **condition** 名 ①(健康)状態, 境遇 ②《-s》状況, 様子
- **conduct** 動 ①指導する ②実施する, 処理[処置]する
- **confectionary** 名 菓子類
- **confectioner** 名 菓子職人, 菓子屋
- **confess** 動 (隠し事などを)告白する, 打ち明ける, 白状する
- **confession** 名 告白, 自白
- **confide** 動 信頼する, 信用する, (秘密などを)打ち明ける
- **confident** 形 自信のある, 自信に満ちた
- **confirm** 動 確かめる, 確かにする
- **confront** 動 ①直面する, 立ち向かう ②突き合わせる, 比較する be confronted with ～に直面している
- **connect** 動 つながる, つなぐ, 関係づける
- **connection** 名 ①つながり, 関係 ②縁故
- **consent** 動 同意する, 承諾する 名 同意, 承諾, 許可
- **consequence** 名 結果, 成り行き in consequence その結果
- **consider** 動 ①考慮する, ～しようと思う ②(～と)みなす ③気にかける, 思いやる
- **considerable** 形 相当な, かなりの, 重要な
- **considerateness** 名 思いやり(深さ)
- **consideration** 名 ①考慮, 考察 ②考慮すべきこと
- **consign** 動 委ねる, 任せる
- **constantly** 副 絶えず, いつも, 絶え間なく
- **construct** 動 建設する, 組み立てる
- **consult** 動 意見を聞く, 相談する
- **consultation** 名 (専門家との)相談, 会議, 診察
- **contain** 動 含む, 入っている
- **contempt** 名 軽蔑, 侮辱, 軽視
- **contrarily** 副 これに反して
- **contrivance** 名 仕掛け
- **convenience** 名 便利(さ), 便利なもの, 利便性
- **conversation** 名 会話, 会談
- **convince** 動 納得させる, 確信させる
- **corpse** 名 (人間の)死体, 死骸
- **correct** 形 正しい, 適切な
- **correctly** 副 正しく, 正確に
- **corridor** 名 廊下
- **cost** 動 (金・費用が)かかる, (～を)要する, (人に金額を)費やさせる
- **costume** 名 衣装, 服装
- **cotton** 名 ①綿, 綿花 ②綿織物, 綿糸
- **could** 熟 How could ～? 何だって～なんてことがありえようか? If +《主語》+ could ～できればなあ《仮定法》could have done ～だったかもしれない《仮定法》
- **counterpart** 名 対応する人[もの] female counterpart 女性の恋人
- **countryman** 名 ①田舎者 ②(ある土地の)出身者, 同郷人
- **couple** 名 ①2つ, 対 ②数個 a couple of 2, 3の
- **courage** 名 勇気, 度胸
- **course** 熟 in due course そのうち, やがて of course もちろん, 当然
- **court** 名 法廷, 裁判所
- **cover** 動 ①覆う, 包む, 隠す ②扱う, (～に)わたる, 及ぶ ③代わりを務め

- る ④補う 名覆い, カバー under separate cover 別封で
- **crab** 名カニ hermit crab ヤドカリ
- **cradle** 名揺りかご
- **craftsman** 名職人, 熟練工
- **cramped** 形窮屈な
- **cranny** 名割れ目 in every nook and cranny あらゆる場所で, 至る所で
- **creak** 動きしむ
- **cream** 名クリーム ice cream アイスクリーム
- **create** 動創造する, 生み出す, 引き起こす
- **creature** 名(神の)創造物, 生物, 動物
- **crepe** 名縮み, ちりめん
- **crime** 名①(法律上の)罪, 犯罪 ②悪事, よくない行為 commit a crime 罪を犯す
- **criminal** 形犯罪の, 罪深い, 恥ずべき 名犯罪者, 犯人
- **cruel** 形残酷な, 厳しい
- **crush** 動押しつぶす, 砕く, 粉々にする
- **cry out** 叫ぶ
- **culprit** 名容疑者, 犯罪者
- **curiosity** 名①好奇心 ②珍しい物[存在]
- **curious** 形好奇心の強い, 珍しい, 奇妙な, 知りたがる
- **curiously** 副①不思議なことに ②もの珍しそうに
- **currently** 副今のところ, 現在
- **curve** 名曲線, カーブ
- **cushion** 名クッション, 背[座]布団 floor cushion 座布団
- **cushioning** 名緩衝材, クッション材
- **customer** 名顧客
- **cut me off** 割り込む, さえぎる

D

- **dagger** 名短剣
- **daily** 形毎日の, 日常の
- **damn** 形ひどい, とんでもない
- **dancer** 名踊り子, ダンサー
- **darkness** 名暗さ, 暗やみ
- **dash** 動①突進する, さっと過ぎ去る ②投げつける dash off 急行する
- **day** all day 一日中, 明けても暮れても one day (過去の)ある日, (未来の)いつか
- **daydream** 名空想, 夢想
- **daze** 名ぼうっとした状態, 当惑すること in a daze 呆然として
- **dead** 熟 better off dead 死んだほうがましだ
- **deal** 名①取引, 扱い ②(不特定の)量, 額 a good [great] deal (of ~) かなり[ずいぶん・大量](の~), 多額(の~)
- **dealer** 名販売人, ディーラー
- **death** 名①死, 死ぬこと ②《the-》終えん, 消滅
- **deceased** 名《the-》故人
- **decidedly** 副きっぱりと, 明らかに
- **declare** 動①宣言する ②断言する ③(税関で)申告する
- **deeply** 副深く, 非常に
- **defense** 名①防御, 守備 ②国防 ③弁護, 弁明
- **definite** 形限定された, 明確な, はっきりした
- **definitely** 副①限定的に, 明確に, 確実に ②まったくそのとおり
- **deft** 形器用な, 手際の良い
- **defy** 動①拒む, 反抗する ②《-+人+to~》…に~しろと挑む

WORD LIST

- **delay** 動 遅らせる, 延期する
- **deliberately** 副 ①故意に, 意図的に ②丹念に, 慎重に
- **delicate** 形 ①繊細な, 壊れやすい ②淡い ③敏感な, きゃしゃな
- **delighted** 形 喜んでいる
- **deliver** 動 配達する, 伝える
- **demanding** 形 要求の厳しい, 注文の多い
- **depend** 動《- on [upon] ~》①~を頼る, ~をあてにする ②~による
- **deposit** 動 置く
- **depressing** 形 落胆させる, 意気消沈させる
- **derby** 名 山高帽
- **derive** 動 ①由来する, 派生する ②(本源から)引き出す ③由来をたどる be derived from ~から生じる
- **description** 名 (言葉で)記述(すること), 描写(すること)
- **desert** 動 見捨てる
- **deserted** 形 人影のない, さびれた
- **deserve** 動 (~を)受けるに足る, 値する, (~して)当然である
- **desire** 名 欲望, 欲求, 願望
- **despite** 前 ~にもかかわらず
- **destine** 動 ①運命づける ②《be - d to》~する運命である be destined for ~に行くことになっている
- **destroy** 動 破壊する, 絶滅させる, 無効にする
- **detail** 名 ①細部, 《-s》詳細 ②《-s》個人情報 動 詳しく述べる
- **detain** 動 引き止める
- **detect** 動 見つける
- **detection** 名 発見, 探知, 検出
- **detective** 名 探偵, 刑事
- **develop** 動 ①発達する[させる] ②開発する
- **devise** 動 工夫する, 考案する
- **devotedly** 形 献身的に, 一心に

- **diagnosis** 名 診断, 分析
- **diet** 名 国会, 議会
- **differ** 動 異なる, 違う, 意見が合わない
- **difficulty** 名 ①むずかしさ ②難局, 支障, 苦情, 異議
- **dig** 動 ①掘る ②小突く ③探る
- **digress** 動 本題からそれる
- **diligently** 副 熱心に, 勤勉に, 念入りに
- **dillydally** 動 ぐずぐずする, のらくらする
- **diplomatic** 形 外交(上)の, 外交官の
- **direct** 形 まっすぐな, 直接の, 率直な, 露骨な 動 (目・注意・努力などを)向ける
- **direction** 名 方向, 方角
- **directly** 副 ①じかに ②まっすぐに ③ちょうど
- **dirt** 名 汚れ, 泥, ごみ dirt floor 土間 dirt poor 赤貧の
- **dirty** 形 汚い, 汚れた
- **disabled** 形 ①無力になった ②身体障害のある
- **disappear** 動 見えなくなる, 姿を消す, なくなる
- **disappointment** 名 失望
- **disassemble** 動 分解する
- **discomfort** 名 不快(なこと), 辛苦, つらさ
- **disconnect** 動 ①(電源・コードなどを)切る, はずす ②関係を絶つ
- **discouragingly** 副 がっかりさせて
- **discovery** 名 発見
- **discuss** 動 議論[検討]する
- **disgraceful** 形 恥ずべき, 不名誉な
- **disgusting** 形 とてもいやな, うんざりさせる, 最低な

Short Stories by Edogawa Ranpo

- **disheveled** 形 〔服装・髪などが〕乱れた, だらしない
- **dismiss** 動 ①解散する ②解雇する ③捨てる ④却下する
- **dismount** 動 取り外す
- **display** 動 展示する, 示す
- **dissipation** 名 浪費, 放蕩, 気晴らし, 娯楽
- **distasteful** 形 不快な, 嫌な
- **distinct** 形 ①独特な ②はっきりした
- **distinguish** 動 ①見分ける, 区別する ②特色づける ③相違を見分ける
- **distract** 動 (注意などを)そらす, まぎらす
- **disturb** 動 かき乱す, 妨げる
- **divide** 動 分かれる, 分ける, 割れる, 割る
- **divine** 動 ～と推測する, ～と思う
- **domain** 名 ①統治地域, 領土 ②領域, 分野
- **don** 動 着用する
- **double** 形 ①2倍の, 二重の ②対の
- **doubly** 副 二重に
- **doubt** 名 ①疑い, 不確かなこと ②未解決点, 困難 no doubt きっと, たぶん 動 疑う
- **down** 熟 up and down 上がったり下がったり, 行ったり来たり, あちこちと
- **downstairs** 副 階下で, 下の部屋で
- **Doyle** 名 (アーサー・コナン・)ドイル《イギリスの小説家》
- **doze** 動 まどろむ, うたた寝する, 居眠りする doze off うつらうつらする, うとうとする
- **drag** 動 ①引きずる ②のろのろ動く[動かす]
- **drain** 動 ①(水が)流れる ②(水が)引く ③水抜きをする, 排出させる
- **drawn** 動 draw (引く)の過去分詞
- **dreadful** 形 恐ろしい
- **dream of** ～を夢見る
- **dreariness** 名 わびしさ, 退屈
- **dreary** 形 荒涼とした, わびしい
- **drift** 動 漂う
- **drunkenly** 副 酔っぱらって, ろれつの回らない口調で
- **due** 形 予定された, 期日のきている, 支払われるべき due to ～によって, ～が原因で in due course そのうち, やがて
- **dug** 動 dig (掘る)の過去, 過去分詞
- **dull** 形 退屈な, 鈍い, くすんだ, ぼんやりした
- **Dupin** 名 (C・オーギュスト・)デュパン《『モルグ街の殺人』の登場人物》
- **dusty** 形 ほこりだらけの
- **dye** 動 染める, 染まる 名 染料

E

- **each other** お互いに
- **earn** 動 ①儲ける, 稼ぐ ②(名声)博す
- **earnestly** 副 まじめに
- **earth** 熟 on earth いったい
- **earth-shattering** 形 あっと驚くような
- **ease** 名 安心, 気楽 at ease のんびりして, 気楽に, くつろいで
- **easily** 副 ①容易に, たやすく, 苦もなく ②気楽に
- **Easy-going** 形 のんきな, 気楽な, のんびりした
- **eaves** 名 軒, ひさし
- **ebonite** 名 硬質ゴム, エボナイト
- **eccentric** 形 常軌を逸した, 普通

WORD LIST

でない

- **Echizen** 名 越前国《かつて日本の地方行政区分だった令制国の一つ》
- **ecstasy** 名 無我夢中, 有頂天, 恍惚, エクスタシー
- **edition** 名 (本・雑誌などの)版
- **effect** 名 影響, 効果, 結果
- **either** 熟 either side of ～の両側に　on either side 両側に
- **eject** 動 追い出す, 立ち退かせる
- **electric** 形 電気の, 電動の
- **elementary** 形 ①初歩の ②単純な, 簡単な
- **eliminate** 動 削除[排除・除去]する, 撤廃する
- **else** 熟 anything else ほかの何か　no one else 他の誰一人として～しない
- **embankment** 名 土手, (護岸)堤防
- **embarrassing** 形 恥ずかしい, きまりが悪い, 当惑させる
- **embrace** 名 抱擁
- **emerge** 動 現れる, 浮かび上がる, 明らかになる
- **emit** 動 ①(におい・光などを)放つ, 放出する ②発行する
- **emotion** 名 感激, 感動, 感情
- **emotional** 形 ①感情の, 心理的な ②感情的な, 感激しやすい
- **emphasis** 名 強調, 強勢, 重要性
- **employee** 名 従業員, 会社員, 被雇用者
- **enable** 動 (～することを)可能にする, 容易にする
- **enact** 動 (法律などを)制定する, 成立させる
- **end** 熟 end up 結局～になる　in the end とうとう, 結局, ついに
- **endeavor** 名 努力
- **endow** 動 寄付する, 授ける, 寄与する　be endowed with ～に恵まれている
- **endure** 動 ①我慢する, 耐え忍ぶ ②持ちこたえる
- **enemy** 名 敵
- **enjoyable** 形 楽しめる, 愉快な
- **enormous** 形 ばく大な, 非常に大きい, 巨大な
- **enough** 熟 sure enough 思ったとおり, 確かに
- **entertain** 動 ①もてなす, 接待する ②楽しませる
- **entertainment** 名 ①楽しみ, 娯楽 ②もてなし, 歓待
- **enthusiastic** 形 熱狂的な, 熱烈な
- **entire** 形 全体の, 完全な, まったくの
- **envelope** 名 封筒, 包み
- **environment** 名 ①環境 ②周囲(の状況), 情勢
- **ephemeral** 形 つかの間の, はかない
- **episode** 名 挿話, 出来事
- **equal** 形 等しい, 均等な, 平等な　be equal to ～に等しい, ～するだけの能力がある
- **equip** 動 備え付ける, 装備する　be equipped to ～の能力がある

- **era** 名 時代, 年代
- **erase** 動 ①消える ②消去する, 抹消する
- **escape** 動 逃げる, 免れる, もれる
- **European** 形 ヨーロッパ(人)の
- **evaluate** 動 ①価値をはかる ②評価する, 査定する
- **even if** たとえ～でも
- **eventually** 副 結局は
- **ever since** それ以来ずっと
- **every time** ～するときはいつも

- □ **everyone** 代誰でも, 皆
- □ **everything** 代すべてのこと[もの], 何でも, 何もかも
- □ **evidence** 名①証拠, 証人 ②形跡
- □ **exact** 形正確な, 厳密な, きちょうめんな
- □ **examination** 名試験, 審査, 検査, 診察
- □ **examine** 動試験する, 調査[検査]する, 診察する
- □ **exceedingly** 副はなはだしく, 非常に
- □ **exception** 名例外, 除外, 異論
- □ **exceptionally** 副例外的に, 特別に, 非常に
- □ **excited** 形興奮した, わくわくした
- □ **excitement** 名興奮(すること)
- □ **excruciatingly** 副耐え難いほどに
- □ **exist** 動存在する, 生存する, ある, いる
- □ **expect** 動予期[予測]する, (当然のこととして)期待する
- □ **expedition** 名遠征, 探検, 遠征[探検]隊
- □ **expel** 動追い出す, 吐き出す, 駆逐する
- □ **experiment** 名実験, 試み
- □ **explanation** 名①説明, 解説, 釈明 ②解釈, 意味
- □ **expose** 動さらす, 露出する
- □ **expression** 名①表現, 表示, 表情 ②言い回し, 語句
- □ **expressionless** 形無表情な
- □ **exquisite** 形この上なくすばらしい, 非常に美しい, 気品のある
- □ **extend** 動①伸ばす, 延長[延期]する ②(範囲が)およぶ, 広がる, (期間などが)わたる
- □ **extraordinarily** 副異常に, 並はずれて, 法外に
- □ **extraordinary** 形異常な, 並はずれた, 驚くべき
- □ **extremely** 副非常に, 極度に
- □ **eye** 熟 keep one's eyes on ～から目をそらさないでいる run one's eyes over ～にザッと目を通す
- □ **eye-catching** 形人目を引く, 目立つ

F

- □ **façade** 名うわべ, 見せ掛け
- □ **face** 熟 face charges for ～で告訴される face to face 面と向かって
- □ **facial** 形顔の, 顔に用いる
- □ **facility** 名①《-ties》施設, 設備 ②器用さ, 容易さ
- □ **fact** as a matter of fact 実際は, 実のところ in fact つまり, 実は, 要するに
- □ **fail** 動①失敗する, 落第する[させる] ②《‐to ～》～し損なう, ～できない ③失望させる
- □ **failure** 名①失敗, 落第 ②不足, 欠乏 ③停止, 減退
- □ **faint** 形かすかな, 弱い, ぼんやりした
- □ **faintly** 副かすかに, ぼんやりと, ほのかに, 力なく
- □ **fall in love with** 恋におちる
- □ **fall to the ground** 転ぶ
- □ **fallen** 動 fall (落ちる)の過去分詞
- □ **familiar** 形①親しい, 親密な ②普通の, いつもの, おなじみの be familiar with ～をよく知っている, ～と親しい
- □ **fantastic** 形空想的な, 奇想天外な, 風変わりな, すばらしい
- □ **fantasy** 名空想, 夢想
- □ **far** 熟 far from ～から遠い, ～どころか far too あまりにも～過ぎる how far どのくらいの距離か so far

WORD LIST

今までのところ、これまでは
- **fat** 形 太った
- **fatal** 形 致命的な、運命を決する
- **fate** 名 運命、宿命 **trick of fate** 運命のいたずら **twist of fate** 運命の意外な展開
- **fear** 動 ①恐れる ②心配する
- **fear-tinged** 形 恐怖の色合いを帯びた
- **fearful** 形 ①恐ろしい ②心配な、気づかって
- **fearless** 形 こわいもの知らずの、大胆な
- **fearsome** 形 恐ろしい、ものすごい
- **feature** 動 ①(～の)特徴になる ②呼び物にする
- **feel** 熟 **not feel like doing** ～する気になれない
- **feeling** 名 ①感じ、気持ち ②触感、知覚 ③同情、思いやり、感受性
- **feet** 熟 **to one's feet** 両足で立っている状態に
- **fellow** 名 ①仲間、同僚 ②人、やつ
- **female** 形 女性の、婦人の、雌の **female counterpart** 女性の恋人
- **fence** 名 囲み、さく
- **ferociously** 副 ひどく、恐ろしく
- **fester** 動 悩ます、痛ませる
- **festivity** 名 行事、にぎわい
- **fiction** 名 フィクション、作り話、小説
- **fierce** 形 どう猛な、荒々しい、すさまじい、猛烈な
- **fiercely** 副 どう猛に、猛烈に
- **figure** 名 ①人[物]の姿、形 ②図(形) ③数字 動 ①描写する、想像する ②計算する ③目立つ、(～として)現れる **figure out** 理解する、～であるとわかる、(原因などを)解明する
- **filled with** 《be-》～でいっぱいになる
- **filly** 名 雌の子馬、お転婆娘
- **filthy** 形 汚い、汚れた、下品な、みだらな
- **final** 形 最後の、決定的な
- **find out** 見つけ出す、気がつく、知る、調べる、解明する
- **finding** 名 ①発見 ②《-s》発見物、調査結果
- **fingernail** 名 指のつめ
- **fingerprint** 名 指紋
- **finished** 形 終わった、仕上がった
- **first** 熟 **first of all** まず第一に **for the first time in one's life** 生まれて初めて
- **firstly** 副 初めに、まず第一に
- **fit** 動 合致[適合]する、合致させる
- **flap** 動 はためく、はためかせる
- **flashlight** 名 懐中電灯、フラッシュ、(灯台などの)回転灯
- **flashy** 形 ①閃光のような ②派手な、けばけばしい
- **fled** 動 flee (逃げる) の過去、過去分詞
- **flee** 動 逃げる、逃亡する
- **flesh** 名 肉、《the-》肉体
- **floor cushion** 座布団
- **flung** 動 fling (投げつける) の過去、過去分詞
- **fold** 動 (手を)組む
- **follow the footsteps of** (人)の足跡をたどる
- **following** 形 《the-》次の、次に続く
- **fondness** 名 好み
- **footing** 名 ①足もと、足どり ②足場、足がかり **with bad footing** 足場の悪い
- **footprint** 名 足型、足跡
- **footstep** 名 足音、歩み **follow the footsteps of** (人)の足跡をたどる
- **force** 名 力、勢い **police force** 警

121

官隊 動①強制する, 力ずくで〜する, 余儀なく〜させる ②押しやる, 押し込む
- **foreboding** 名 (悪いことが起きる) 予感, (不吉な) 前兆
- **foreign-run** 形 外国資本の, 外資系の
- **foreigner** 名 外国人, 外国製品
- **foreleg** 名 (四足動物の) 前脚
- **forgive** 動 許す, 免除する
- **forgiveness** 名 許す (こと), 寛容
- **form** 名 ①形, 形式 ②書式 動 形づくる
- **formality** 名 ①形式的であること, 儀礼 (的行為), 形式的手続き ②正規の手続き
- **forte** 名 強み, 長所
- **fortunately** 幸運にも
- **foul** 形 悪臭のある, 不潔な, 汚い, ひどい
- **foul-smelling** 形 悪臭のする
- **fragrance** 名 芳香
- **frame** 名 骨組み, 構造, 額縁
- **frankness** 名 率直さ
- **freakish** 形 奇妙な, 気まぐれな
- **friend of mine** 《a-》友人の1人
- **friendly** 形 親しみのある, 親切な, 友情のこもった
- **friendship** 名 友人であること, 友情
- **frightened** 形 おびえた, びっくりした
- **frightening** 形 恐ろしい, どきっとさせる
- **fringed** 形 房 (飾り) の付いた, 縁のある fringed pink 撫子《植物》
- **fro** 熟 to and fro あちこちに, 行ったり来たり
- **front** 熟 in front of 〜の前に, 〜の正面に
- **frontage** 名 (建物の) 正面, 間口

- **fulfill** 動 (義務・約束を) 果たす, (要求・条件を) 満たす
- **full of** 《be-》〜でいっぱいである
- **funny** 形 ①おもしろい, こっけいな ②奇妙な, うさんくさい
- **furniture** 名 家具, 備品, 調度
- **further** 形 いっそう遠い, その上の, なおいっそうの 副 いっそう遠く, その上に, もっと
- **furthermore** 副 さらに, その上

G

- **galvanize** 動 奮い立たせる, 駆り立てる
- **gap** 名 ギャップ, 隔たり, すき間
- **gasp** 動 ①あえぐ ②はっと息をのむ
- **gather** 動 ①集まる, 集める ②生じる, 増す ③推測する
- **gaudy** 形 派手な, けばけばしい
- **gaunt** 形 痩せこけた, やつれた
- **gaze** 名 凝視, 注視 turn one's gaze away 目をそらす
- **genius** 名 天才, 才能
- **gently** 副 親切に, 上品に, そっと, 優しく
- **genuine** 形 ①本物の ②心からの
- **get** 熟 get 〜 across 〜を伝える get at 〜を目指す, ほのめかす get close to 〜に近づく, 接近する get on 進行する get out of 〜から外へ出る [抜け出る] get over 乗り越える get the upper hand 勝つ get to (事) を始める, 〜に達する [到着する] get to do 〜できるようになる, 〜できる機会を得る get under way 始まる
- **geta** 名 下駄
- **ghastly** 副 ぞっとする, 恐ろしい
- **gift** 名 ①贈り物 ②(天賦の) 才能

WORD LIST

- **give a start** びくっとする
- **give it a shot** 一丁やってみる
- **give up** あきらめる, やめる, 引き渡す
- **gleam** 動 (かすかに)光る
- **glimpse** 名 ちらりと見ること catch a glimpse 一目見る
- **go** 熟 go around and around in someone's head 〔考えや悩みなどが〕(人)の頭の中をグルグルと回る go back to ~に帰る[戻る], ~に遡る, (中断していた作業に)再び取り掛かる go by ①(時が)過ぎる, 経過する ②~のそばを通る ③~に基づいて[よって]行う go down 下に降りる go in 中に入る, 開始する go into ~に入る go on 続く, 続ける, 進み続ける, 起こる, 発生する go out 外出する, 外へ出る go over ~を越えて行く, ~へ渡る go through 通り抜ける, 一つずつ順番に検討する go up to ~まで行く, 近づく let go of ~から手を離す
- **going concern** 継続企業
- **good** 熟 be good at ~が得意だ do ~ good ~のためになる
- **gossip** 名 うわさ話, ゴシップ 動 うわさ話をする, 雑談する
- **got to** ~しなければならない
- **gotten** 動 get (得る)の過去分詞
- **Göttingen** 名 ゲッティンゲン《ドイツの都市名》
- **governor** 名 知事
- **gradually** 副 だんだんと
- **grant** 動 ①許可する, 承諾する ②授与する, 譲渡する ③(なるほどと)認める
- **gratefully** 副 感謝を込めて
- **grave** 形 重要な, 厳粛な, 落ち着いた
- **graven** 形 心[記憶]に刻まれた
- **great deal** 多量に, 大いに, ずっと
- **Greek** 形 ギリシア(人・語)の

- **greeting** 名 あいさつ(の言葉), あいさつ(状)
- **grey** 形 灰色の
- **grossly** 形 極めて, ひどく
- **ground** 熟 fall to the ground 転ぶ
- **grow to** ~するようになる
- **growl** 動 (~に向かって)うなる, 不平を言う, どなる
- **grudge** 名 うらみ hold a grudge against (人)を恨む
- **guard** 名 ①警戒, 見張り ②番人 off guard (人が)警戒を怠って, 油断して
- **guest** 名 客, ゲスト
- **guffaw** 動 ばか笑いする

H

- **ha** 間 ほう, まあ, おや《驚き・悲しみ・不満・喜び・笑い声などを表す》
- **habit** 名 習慣, 癖, 気質
- **habitat** 名 ①生息地 ②たまり場
- **hairy** 形 毛むくじゃらの, 毛製の
- **Hakuryu, Kanda** 神田伯龍《講釈師》
- **halfway** 副 中間[中途]で
- **hall** 名 公会堂, ホール, 大広間, 玄関
- **hammer** 動 ハンマーで打つ
- **hand** 熟 at hand 目の前にある hand over 手渡す, 引き渡す, 譲渡する
- **handcart** 名 手車
- **handkerchief** 名 ハンカチ
- **handsome** 形 端正な(顔立ちの), りっぱな, (男性が)ハンサムな
- **hang** 動 かかる, かける, つるす, ぶら下がる hang on じっと聞いている, 一心に聞く hang up 中断する
- **happen to** たまたま~する, 偶然

- ~する
- **happy to do** 《be-》~してうれしい, 喜んで~する
- **harass** 動 悩ます, 苦しめる, いやがらせる
- **hard to** ~し難い
- **hardly** 副 ①ほとんど~でない, わずかに ②厳しく, かろうじて
- **hardtack** 名 乾パン
- **harmonious** 形 調和のとれた, 仲むつまじい
- **hastily** 副 急いで, 軽率に
- **have** 熟 could have done ~だったかもしれない《仮定法》 have no choice but to ~するしかない have no idea わからない should have done ~すべきだった(のにしなかった)《仮定法》 will have done ~してしまっているだろう《未来完了形》
- **head** 熟 go around and around in someone's head〔考えや悩みなどが〕(人)の頭の中をグルグルと回る
- **headline** 名 (新聞などの)見出し
- **hear of** ~について聞く
- **heat** 名 熱, 暑さ
- **height** 名 高さ, 身長
- **heinous** 形 凶悪な
- **hell** 名 地獄, 地獄のようなところ[状態]
- **help** 熟 cannot help ~ing ~せずにはいられない
- **here and there** あちこちで
- **hermit** 名 隠者, 世捨て人 hermit crab ヤドカリ
- **hesitant** 形 ちゅうちょする, ためらいがちな
- **hidden** 動 hide (隠れる)の過去分詞
- **hide** 動 隠れる, 隠す, 隠れて見えない, 秘密にする hide out 潜伏している

- **hideous** 形 ひどくみにくい, ぞっとする
- **hideously** 副 恐ろしいほどに
- **hidey-hole** 名 隠し穴, 潜伏場所
- **high-minded** 形 気高い
- **high-quality** 形 高品質の
- **highly** 副 ①大いに, 非常に ②高度に, 高位に ③高く評価して, 高価で
- **hinged** 形 ヒンジ[蝶番]で連結された hinged door 開き戸
- **Hirokoji in Ueno** 上野広小路《地名》
- **hit upon** ~を思いつく
- **hold a grudge against** (人)を恨む
- **hold one's own** 引けを取らない
- **hollow** 形 うつろな, くぼんだ
- **Holmes** (シャーロック・)ホームズ《小説家アーサー・コナン・ドイルによる, シャーロック・ホームズシリーズの主人公》
- **home** 熟 on one's way home 帰り道で
- **hometown** 名 ①生まれ故郷, 出身地 ②現在住んでいる町
- **honest** 形 ①正直な, 誠実な, 心からの ②公正な, 感心な
- **honesty** 名 正直, 誠実
- **hopelessly** 副 希望を失って, どうしようもなく
- **horrible** 形 恐ろしい, ひどい
- **host** 名 客をもてなす主人
- **housewife** 名 主婦
- **hover** 動 うろつく
- **how** 熟 How about ~? ~はどうですか。~しませんか。 How could ~? 何だって~なんてことがありえようか? how far どのくらいの距離か no matter how どんなに~であろうとも

Word List

- **however** 副 たとえ～でも 接 けれども, だが
- **hug** 動 しっかりと抱き締める
- **human being** 人, 人間
- **humanity** 名 人間性, 人間らしさ
- **humbly** 副 謙虚に, 謹んで
- **hung** 動 hang (かかる) の過去, 過去分詞
- **hurry** 熟 hurry up 急ぐ in a hurry 急いで, あわてて
- **hypnotically** 副 催眠にかかったように
- **hysterical** 形 ヒステリックな, ヒステリー症の

I

- **ice cream** アイスクリーム
- **iced coffee** アイスコーヒー
- **idea** 熟 have no idea わからない
- **ideal** 形 理想的な, 申し分のない
- **identify** 動 ①(本人・同一と)確認する, 見分ける ②意気投合する
- **idler** 名 怠け者, 役立たず
- **if** 熟 as if あたかも～のように, まるで～みたいに ask ～ if ～かどうか尋ねる even if たとえ～でも If+《主語》+ could ～できればなあ《仮定法》 if possible できるなら wonder if ～ではないかと思う
- **ignore** 動 無視する, 怠る
- **illusion** 名 ①錯覚, 幻想 ②勘違い, 見間違い
- **image** 名 ①印象, 姿 ②画像, 映像
- **imagination** 名 想像(力), 空想
- **imagine** 動 想像する, 心に思い描く
- **imitate** 動 まねる, 模造する
- **immediately** 副 すぐに, ～するやいなや

- **impact** 名 影響力, 反響, 効果
- **impassioned** 形 情熱の込もった
- **imperceptibly** 副 わずかに, かすかに
- **impertinent** 形 尊大な, 生意気な, 不作法な
- **impression** 名 ①印象, 感想 ②感動
- **inanimate** 形 生気のない, 生命のない
- **inasmuch as** ～だから, ～なので
- **inaudible** 形 聞き取れない
- **incident** 名 出来事, 事故, 事変, 紛争
- **including** 前 ～を含めて, 込みで
- **inconvenience** 名 不便, 不自由
- **incredible** 形 ①信じられない, 信用できない ②すばらしい, とてつもない
- **indeed** 副 ①実際, 本当に ②《強意》まったく
- **indescribable** 形 言葉で言い表せない, 言語に絶する
- **indescribably** 形 言葉では言い表せないほど
- **India** 名 インド《国名》
- **indirect** 形 間接的な, 二次的な
- **individual** 形 独立した, 個性的な, 個々の
- **individually** 副 個人的に, 1つひとつ
- **indulge** 動 ①満足する[させる], 甘やかす ②ふける, 従事する
- **inexplicable** 形 説明し難い, 不可解
- **infatuated** 形 夢中になった be infatuated with ～に夢中になる
- **inferior** 形 (質の) 劣った, 下位の, 粗悪な
- **inferiority** 名 劣っていること, 劣等

125

- ☐ **inflict** 動 (相手にとって嫌なこと・苦痛になることを)押し付ける、(人)に重荷を負わせる
- ☐ **inform** 動 ①告げる、知らせる ②密告する
- ☐ **inhibition** 名 禁止、抑制
- ☐ **ink** 名 インク
- ☐ **inkling** 名 うすうす感づくこと
- ☐ **inkstone** 名 すずり(硯)
- ☐ **inn** 名 宿屋、居酒屋
- ☐ **inner** 形 ①内部の ②心の中の
- ☐ **innocence** 名 ①無邪気、純真 ②無罪、潔白
- ☐ **innocent** 形 無邪気な、無実の
- ☐ **inquiry** 名 ①質問、探求、問い合わせ ②事実を求めること
- ☐ **insane** 形 正気でない、狂気の
- ☐ **inscription** 名 刻みつけること、銘
- ☐ **insight** 名 洞察、真相、見識
- ☐ **insolence** 名 横柄[無礼](な言動)
- ☐ **inspect** 動 検査する、調べる
- ☐ **inspector** 名 (英国の)警部補
  chief inspector 警察署の司法主任
- ☐ **inspire** 動 ①奮い立たせる、鼓舞する ②(感情などを)吹き込む ③霊感を与える
- ☐ **install** 動 ①取り付ける ②任命する
- ☐ **instance** 名 ①例 ②場合、事実
  for instance たとえば
- ☐ **instant** 名 瞬間、寸時
- ☐ **instead** 副 その代わりに
- ☐ **instigate** 動 〜を駆り立てる
- ☐ **intelligent** 形 頭のよい、聡明な
- ☐ **intend** 動《 – to 〜》〜しようと思う、〜するつもりである
- ☐ **intensity** 名 強烈さ、激しさ
- ☐ **intently** 副 熱心に
- ☐ **interested** 形 興味を持った、関心のある
- ☐ **interesting** 形 おもしろい、興味を起こさせる
- ☐ **interior** 名 内部、室内、インテリア
- ☐ **interpret** 動 ①通訳する ②説明する ③解釈する
- ☐ **interrogate** 動 (人)に問いただす、根掘り葉掘り尋ねる、尋問する
- ☐ **interrogation** 名 質問、尋問、審問
- ☐ **interrupt** 動 さえぎる、妨害する、口をはさむ
- ☐ **intoxicating** 形 夢中にさせる
- ☐ **invent** 動 ①発明[考案]する ②ねつ造する
- ☐ **invention** 名 ①発明(品) ②作り事、でっち上げ
- ☐ **inventory** 名 全ての物のリスト[一覧表]
- ☐ **investigate** 動 研究する、調査する、捜査する
- ☐ **investigation** 名 (徹底的な)調査、取り調べ
- ☐ **investigator** 名 調査者、捜査官、研究員
- ☐ **invisibility** 名 不可視性、目に見えないこと
- ☐ **invisible** 形 目に見えない、表に出ない
- ☐ **involuntarily** 副 ①思わず、無意識に ②不本意ながら、心ならずも
- ☐ **involve** 動 ①含む、伴う ②巻き込む、かかわらせる
- ☐ **ironic** 形 皮肉な、反語的な
- ☐ **irrefutable** 形 反論できない
- ☐ **item** 名 ①項目、品目 ②(新聞などの)記事
- ☐ **itself** 代 それ自体、それ自身

J

- ☐ **jabbering** 名 他愛もないおしゃべり

- **jacket** 名 ①短い上着 ②(書物などの)カバー
- **jangle** 動 ①じゃんじゃん鳴らす ②いらだたせる
- **Japan** 名 日本《国名》
- **Japanese** 形 日本(人・語)の 名 ①日本人 ②日本語
- **Japanese-run** 形 日本人経営の
- **Japanese-style** 形 和風の
- **jewel** 名 宝石, 貴重な人[物]
- **jiggle** 動 軽く揺れる
- **join in** 加わる, 参加する
- **jolt** 名 急な揺れ, ショック
- **jostle** 動 ~を(乱暴に)押す, 突く
- **jot** 動 さっと書き留める, メモする jot down 手早くメモする
- **joy** 名 喜び, 楽しみ
- **judge** 動 判決を下す, 裁く, 判断する, 評価する 名 裁判官, 判事, 審査員
- **judgment** 名 ①判断, 意見 ②裁判, 判決
- **jumble** 名 ごちゃ混ぜ, 混乱
- **jump on** ~に飛びかかる
- **jurist** 名 法学者, 法律専門家
- **just as** (ちょうど)であろうとおり
- **just then** そのとたんに
- **justify** 動 正しいとする, 弁明する

K

- **Kanda Hakuryu** 神田伯龍《講釈師》
- **keep on ~ing** ~し続ける, 繰り返し~する
- **khaki** 形 カーキ地[色]の
- **kimono** 名 着物
- **kind to** 《be-》~に親切である
- **kind of** ある程度, いくらか, ~のようなもの[人] all kinds of さまざまな, あらゆる種類の
- **kindly** 副 親切に, 優しく
- **kiss** 動 キスする
- **kitten** 名 子猫
- **knack** 名 こつ, 要領, 才覚
- **knee** 名 ひざ
- **know** 熟 as you know ご存知のとおり know of ~について知っている
- **knowing** 形 物知りの, 故意の
- **knowledge** 名 知識, 理解, 学問
- **known as** 《be-》~として知られている
- **Kobayashi** 名 小林《人名》

L

- **laborer** 名 労働者
- **lack** 動 不足している, 欠けている 名 不足, 欠乏
- **lap** 名 ひざ
- **largely** 副 大いに, 主として
- **last** 熟 at last ついに, とうとう
- **late for** 《be-》~に遅れる
- **lately** 副 近ごろ, 最近
- **latest** 形 最新の, 最近の
- **lattice** 名 格子
- **lattice-like** 形 格子状の
- **laugh at** ~を見て[聞いて]笑う
- **laughter** 名 笑い(声)
- **lavatory** 名 洗面所, 手洗い
- **lavishly** 副 気前よく, 惜しげなく
- **lay** 動 lie (横たわる)の過去 lie dead 死んで横たわる
- **layer** 名 層, 重ね
- **layperson** 名 素人
- **laze** 動 怠けて[ぼんやりと]過ごす laze around のらくら過ごす
- **lead** 名 手がかり

- [ ] **lean** 動 ①もたれる, 寄りかかる ② 傾く, 傾ける 形 やせた
- [ ] **least** 形 いちばん小さい, 最も少ない 名 最小, 最少 **at least** 少なくとも
- [ ] **leather** 名 皮革, 皮製品
- [ ] **leather-covered** 形 (ソファなどが) 革張りの
- [ ] **leather-sheathed** 形 革に覆われた
- [ ] **leave behind** あとにする, 〜を置き去りにする
- [ ] **leave in** 〜をそのままにしておく
- [ ] **lecherous** 形 好色な
- [ ] **legitimate** 形 合法の, 合法的な
- [ ] **leisure** 名 余暇 **at leisure** 暇で, ゆっくり
- [ ] **length** 名 長さ, 縦, たけ, 距離 **at length** ついに, 長々と, 詳しく
- [ ] **Leroux** 名 (ガストン・) ルルー《フランスの小説家》
- [ ] **less** 副 〜より少なく, 〜ほどでなく
- [ ] **let alone** まして〜なんて (ない)
- [ ] **Let me see.** ええと。
- [ ] **let go of** 〜から手を離す
- [ ] **let us** どうか私たちに〜させてください
- [ ] **liable** 形 〜しやすい, 〜しがちの
- [ ] **liberty** 名 ①自由, 解放 ②《-ties》特権, 特典 ③《-ties》勝手な振る舞い
- [ ] **lie** 動 ①うそをつく ②横たわる, 寝る ③(ある状態に)ある, 存在する 名 うそ, 詐欺
- [ ] **life** 熟 **for the first time in one's life** 生まれて初めて
- [ ] **light bulb** 電球
- [ ] **lightly** 副 ①軽く, そっと ②軽率に
- [ ] **like** 熟 **like this** このような, こんなふうに **look like** 〜のように見える, 〜に似ている **not feel like doing** 〜する気になれない
- [ ] **likely** 副 たぶん, おそらく
- [ ] **liking** 名 好み, 趣味
- [ ] **limit** 動 〜を限定[制限]する
- [ ] **linger** 動 長居する, 後まで残る, ぐずぐずする
- [ ] **lip** 名 唇, 《-s》口
- [ ] **lit** 動 light (火をつける) の過去, 過去分詞
- [ ] **living** 名 生計, 生活 形 ①生きている, 現存の ②居住用の
- [ ] **load** 動 (荷を) 積む
- [ ] **loan** 動 貸す
- [ ] **loathsome** 形 ひどく不快な, 忌まわしい
- [ ] **lobby** 名 ロビー, (玄関) 広間
- [ ] **locate** 動 置く, 居住する[させる]
- [ ] **lodging** 名 ①宿泊, 宿 ②《-s》下宿
- [ ] **logically** 副 論理的に
- [ ] **lonely** 形 ①孤独な, 心さびしい ②ひっそりした, 人里離れた
- [ ] **long** 熟 **before long** やがて, まもなく **take long** 時間がかかる
- [ ] **longer** 熟 **no longer** もはや〜でない [〜しない]
- [ ] **look** 熟 **look around** まわりを見回す **look back at** 〜に視線を戻す, 〜を振り返って見る **look for** 〜を探す **look into** 〜を調査する **look like** 〜のように見える, 〜に似ている **look on** 傍観する, 眺める **look over** 〜越しに見る, 〜を見る **look up** 見上げる, 調べる **take a look at** 〜をちょっと見る
- [ ] **loss** 名 ①損失(額・物), 損害, 浪費 ②失敗, 敗北
- [ ] **lot** 名 区画
- [ ] **loudly** 副 大声で, 騒がしく
- [ ] **lounge** 名 ラウンジ, 休憩室
- [ ] **love** 熟 **fall in love with** 恋におちる
- [ ] **lover** 名 ①愛人, 恋人 ②愛好者

WORD LIST

- **low-level** 形 低レベルの, 下層の
- **lower** 動 下げる, 低くする
- **luck** 熟 push one's luck 調子に乗りすぎる
- **luckily** 副 運よく, 幸いにも
- **ludicrous** 形 ひどく滑稽な, ばかげた
- **lump** 名 ①(固くて小さな)かたまり ②こぶ, はれ
- **luscious** 形 (男性にとって)官能的な, そそられる
- **lust** 名 熱情, 欲望, 色情, 強い性欲
- **luxuriantly** 副 豊かに
- **luxury** 形 豪華な, 高級な, 贅沢な 名 豪華さ, 贅沢(品)
- **lying** 動 lie (うそをつく・横たわる) の現在分詞

M

- **mad** 形 ①気の狂った ②逆上した, 理性をなくした ③ばかげた ④(〜に)熱狂[熱中]して, 夢中の
- **madam** 名《ていねいな呼びかけ》奥様, お嬢様
- **made up of**《be –》〜で構成されている
- **maggot** 名 うじ虫
- **magician** 名 魔法使い, 奇術師, マジシャン
- **magnificent** 形 壮大な, 壮麗な, すばらしい
- **maid** 名 お手伝い, メイド
- **main** 形 主な, 主要な
- **major** 形 大きいほうの, 主な, 一流の
- **majority** 名 ①大多数, 大部分 ②過半数
- **make a round of** あちこちの〜を訪れる
- **make over** 譲り渡す
- **make up** 作り出す, 考え出す, 〜を構成[形成]する make up one's mind 決心する
- **make use of** 〜を利用する, 〜を生かす
- **make ~ into** 〜を…に仕立てる
- **maker** 名 作る人, メーカー
- **male** 形 男の, 雄の
- **malice** 名 悪意, 敵意
- **manage** 動 ①動かす, うまく処理する ②経営[管理]する, 支配する ③どうにか〜する
- **manager** 名 経営者, 支配人, 支店長, 部長
- **manner** 名 ①方法, やり方 ②態度, 様子 ③《-s》行儀, 作法, 生活様式
- **mansion** 名 大邸宅
- **manuscript** 名 原稿, 手書き原稿, 写本
- **many-colored** 形 色とりどりの, 多色の
- **mark** 名 印, 記号, 跡
- **Marquis de Sade** サド侯爵《フランスの小説家。異常な性を描きサディズムの語を生んだ》
- **marriage** 名 結婚(生活・式)
- **marvelous** 形 驚くべき, 驚嘆すべき, すばらしい
- **Masoch** 名 (ザッヘル)マゾッホ《オーストリアの小説家。被虐的な異常性欲を描きマゾヒズムの語を生んだ》
- **masochism** 名 マゾヒズム, 被虐症
- **mass-market** 形 大衆市場の
- **master** 名 主人, 雇い主, 師, 名匠
- **masterful** 形 優れた技量の
- **mat** 名 マット, 敷物
- **match** 名 相手, 釣り合うもの 動 調和する, 釣り合う
- **materialist** 名 ①唯物論[主義]者 ②物質[実利]主義者

- **matter** 熟 a matter of ～の問題 as a matter of fact 実際は、実のところ no matter how どんなに～であろうとも no matter what たとえ何があろう[起ころう]と
- **May I ～?** ～してもよいですか。
- **mean** 熟 I do not mean to ～するつもりはないのですが
- **means** 熟 by no means 決して～ではない means of ～する手段
- **measure** 動 ①測る、(～の)寸法がある ②評価する
- **meatiness** 名 肉付きのよさ
- **mechanical** 形 機械の、機械的な
- **medical** 形 医学の medical officer 警察医
- **meet with** ～に出会う
- **meeting** 名 集まり、ミーティング、面会
- **memory** 名 記憶(力)、思い出
- **mention** 動 (～について)述べる、言及する 名 言及、陳述
- **mere** 形 単なる、ほんの、まったく～にすぎない
- **messenger** 名 使者、(伝言・小包などの)配達人、伝達者
- **method** 名 ①方法、手段 ②秩序、体系
- **metropolis** 名 首都、大都市、メトロポリス
- **middle** 名 中間、最中 in the middle of ～の真ん中[最中]に
- **midnight** 名 夜の12時、真夜中
- **midst** 名 真ん中、中央
- **might** 《mayの過去》①～かもしれない ②～してもよい、～できる 名 力、権力
- **mile** 名 ①マイル《長さの単位。1,609m》②《-s》かなりの距離 Something Mile Road 何間道路とかいう大通り
- **mimic** 動 まねをする
- **mind** 名 ①心、精神、考え ②知性 make up one's mind 決心する 動 ①気にする、いやがる ②気をつける、用心する
- **mind-boggling** 形 あぜんとさせる、度肝を抜かれる
- **mine** 熟 a friend of mine 友人の1人
- **minute** 熟 Wait a minute. ちょっと待って。
- **miserable** 形 みじめな、哀れな
- **misery** 名 ①悲惨、みじめさ ②苦痛、不幸、苦難
- **mistaken** 動 mistake (間違える)の過去分詞 形 誤った
- **mistook** 動 mistake (間違える)の過去
- **mistreatment** 名 (人に対する)不当な扱い、虐待
- **mistress** 名 ①愛人、恋人 ②女主人、女性の支配者、女性の先生
- **mix** 動 ①混ざる、混ぜる ②(～を)一緒にする
- **modest** 形 控えめな、謙虚な
- **moment** 名 ①瞬間、ちょっとの間 ②(特定の)時、時期 at that moment その時に、その瞬間に for a moment 少しの間
- **monotony** 名 単調さ、一本調子、退屈さ
- **monster** 名 怪物
- **morally** 副 道徳的に、事実上
- **more** 熟 more and more ますます more of ～よりもっと more than ～以上 no more than ただの～にすぎない once more もう一度
- **moreover** 副 その上、さらに
- **motivate** 動 動機付ける、刺激する
- **move in** 引っ越す
- **movement** 名 ①動き、運動 ②《-s》行動 ③引っ越し ④変動

WORD LIST

- **much** 腦 as much as ～と同じだけ　not so much as ～ほどではない　too much 過度の
- **muddy** 形 泥だらけの，ぬかるみの
- **Munsterberg** 名 （ヒューゴー・）ミュンスターベルヒ《ドイツ出身のアメリカの心理学者，哲学者》
- **murder** 名 人殺し，殺害，殺人事件 動 殺す
- **murderer** 名 殺人犯
- **Murders in the Rue Morgue** 『モルグ街の殺人』《エドガー・アラン・ポーによる短編推理小説》
- **muso** 名 無窓《障子で普通，紙を貼るべき中央部分が細かい縦の二重の格子になっていて開閉できる》
- **mysterious** 形 神秘的な，謎めいた
- **mystery** 名 ①神秘，不可思議 ②推理小説，ミステリー
- **Mystery of the Yellow Room** 『黄色い部屋の秘密』《ガストン・ルルー作の推理小説》

N

- **nail** 名 ①爪 ②くぎ，びょう
- **naked** 形 裸の，むき出しの
- **nape** 名 襟首，首筋
- **narrow** 形 ①狭い ②限られた 動 狭くなる[する]
- **nasal** 形 鼻の
- **native** 形 出生(地)の，自国の
- **naturally** 副 生まれつき，自然に，当然
- **nay** 副 否，いや
- **nearby** 副 近くで，間近で
- **nearly** 副 ①近くに，親しく ②ほとんど，あやうく
- **necessarily** 副 ①必ず，必然的に，やむを得ず ②《not ～》必ずしも～でない
- **necktie** 名 ネクタイ
- **Negro** 名 黒人《歴史的文脈以外では蔑称》
- **neighborhood** 名 近所(の人々)，付近
- **neither** 形 どちらの～も…でない 代 (2者のうち)どちらも～でない 副 《否定文に続いて》～も…しない　neither ～ nor … ～も…もない
- **nerve** 名 ①神経 ②気力，精力
- **nestle** 動 （～に）気持ちよく横たわる，身を落ち着ける
- **nevertheless** 副 それにもかかわらず，それでもやはり
- **news** 名 報道，ニュース，便り，知らせ
- **newspaper** 名 新聞(紙)
- **next to** ～のとなりに，～の次に
- **nightly** 形 夜ごとの
- **nightmare** 名 悪夢
- **nincompoopish** 形 間抜けな
- **no one** 誰も[一人も]～ない　no one else 他の誰一人として～しない
- **noble** 形 気高い，高貴な，りっぱな，高貴な
- **nobleman** 名 貴族，高貴の生まれの人
- **nobody** 代 誰も[1人も]～ない
- **nod** 動 うなずく，うなずいて～を示す
- **noise** 名 騒音，騒ぎ，物音
- **noisily** 副 音を立てて，騒々しく
- **nonchalantly** 副 無関心に，平然と，のほほんと
- **nonetheless** 副 それでもなお，それにもかかわらず
- **nonsense** 名 ばかげたこと，ナンセンス
- **nook** 名 隅，奥まった個所　in

- **every nook and cranny** あらゆる場所で, 至る所で
- **nor** 接 ～もまたない
- **nor** 熟 Nor do I. 《否定の文に続けて》私も(いや)です。 neither ～ nor … ～も…もない
- **normal** 形 普通の, 平均の, 標準的な
- **normally** 副 普通は, 通常は
- **nose** 熟 right under one's nose 目と鼻の先に
- **note** 動 ①書き留める ②注意[注目]する
- **notebook** 名 ノート, 手帳
- **nothing but** ただ～だけ, ～にすぎない, ～のほかは何も…ない
- **notice** 名 ①注意 ②通知 ③公告 動 ①気づく, 認める ②通告する
- **novel** 名 (長編)小説
- **now that** 今や～だから, ～からには
- **now-bright** 今や明るくなった
- **nowhere** 副 どこにも～ない
- **numb** 動 無感覚にする, 麻痺させる
- **number of** 《a –》いくつかの～, 多くの～
- **numerous** 形 多数の
- **nursemaid** 名 子守り女

O

- **object** 名 ①物, 事物 ②目的物, 対象
- **objective** 名 目標, 目的
- **oblivious** 形 忘れている, 気にしない
- **observation** 名 観察(力), 注目
- **observe** 動 ①観察[観測]する, 監視[注視]する ②気づく ③守る, 遵守する
- **observer** 名 観察者, オブザーバー
- **obsessive** 形 強迫観念[妄想]に駆られた, 執拗な, 異常な
- **obsessively** 副 しつようにに, 異常なほど
- **obviously** 副 明らかに, はっきりと
- **occasion** 名 ①場合, (特定の)時 ②機会, 好機 ③理由, 根拠
- **occasionally** 副 時折, 時たま
- **occur** 動 (事が)起こる, 生じる, (考えなどが)浮かぶ
- **odd** 形 ①奇妙な ②奇数の ③(一対のうちの)片方の
- **oddly** 副 奇妙なことに
- **of course** もちろん, 当然
- **off guard** (人が)警戒を怠って, 油断して
- **off to** ～へ出かける
- **offend** 動 ①感情を害する ②罪を犯す, 反する
- **offer** 動 申し出る, 申し込む, 提供する
- **officer** 名 役人, 公務員, 警察官 medical officer 警察医
- **oil painting** 油絵
- **omit** 動 除外する, 怠る
- **On the Road** 『途上』《小説。谷崎潤一郎著》
- **On the Witness Stand** 『心理学と犯罪』《書名。ミュンスターベルヒ著》
- **once** 熟 at once すぐに, 同時に once more もう一度
- **one another** お互い
- **one day** (過去の)ある日, (未来の)いつか
- **one side** 片側
- **oneself** 代 自分自身 by oneself 自分だけで for oneself 独力で, 自分のために

Word List

- **onlooker** 名 傍観者, やじ馬
- **only** 熟 not only ~ but (also) … ~だけでなく…もまた
- **onward** 副 前方へ, 進んで from ~ onward ~以降
- **Ooka** 名 大岡忠相《江戸時代中期の幕臣・大名》
- **open up** 広がる, 広げる, 開く, 開ける
- **opportunity** 名 好機, 適当な時期[状況]
- **opposite** 形 反対の, 向こう側の 前 ~の向こう側に
- **opt** 動 選ぶ, 選択する
- **opulent** 形 (量が)豊富な, たっぷりの, 豪勢な
- **orangutan** 名 オランウータン
- **ordain** 動 (神や運命が)定める, 運命づける
- **order** 熟 in order to ~するために, ~しようと
- **ordinarily** 副 ①通常は ②普通に, 人並みに
- **ordinary** 形 ①普通の, 通常の ②並の, 平凡な
- **orientation** 名 方針, オリエンテーション, 適応
- **original** 形 始めの, 元の, 本来の
- **other** 熟 each other お互いに in other words すなわち, 言い換えれば
- **out** 熟 be out 外出している out of ①~から外へ, ~から抜け出して ②~から作り出して, ~を材料として ③~の範囲外に, ~から離れて ④(ある数)の中から out ot the blue 突然
- **outdoors** 名 《the-》戸外, 野外
- **outlandish** 形 風変わりな, 異様な, 奇妙な
- **outlet** 名 出口
- **outrageous** 形 怒り狂った, 極悪な, 乱暴な, とんでもない
- **outskirts** 名 郊外, はずれ
- **over** 熟 all over 全体に亘って be over 終わる over there あそこに
- **overall** 形 総体的な, 全面的な
- **overcame** 動 overcome (勝つ)の過去
- **overcome** 動 勝つ, 打ち勝つ, 克服する
- **overlay** 動 かぶせる, 覆う, 重ね合わせる
- **overlook** 動 見落とす, (チャンスなどを)逃す
- **overpowering** 形 (人の性格が)威圧的な, 高飛車な
- **overshadow** 動 ~に影を投げ掛ける, 見劣りさせる
- **overstep** 動 (境界線・制限などを)越える
- **overture** 名 申し入れ, 予備(的)交渉, 序曲, 序章
- **overwhelmed** 形 圧倒された, 参った, 困惑した
- **own** 熟 of one's own 自分自身の on one's own 自力で
- **owner** 名 持ち主, オーナー

P

- **painting** 名 絵, 絵画, 油絵
- **pair** 名 (2つから成る)一対, 一組, ペア
- **pale** 形 (顔色・人が)青ざめた, 青白い
- **paneled** 形 パネル張りの
- **panic** 名 パニック, 恐慌
- **Paris** 名 パリ《フランスの首都》
- **part** 熟 play a part 役目を果たす
- **particular** 形 ①特別の ②詳細な 名 事項, 細部,《-s》詳細 in particular 特に, とりわけ

- **particularly** 副 特に, とりわけ
- **partly** 副 一部分は, ある程度は
- **pass by** ～のそばを通る［通り過ぎる］
- **pass down** (次の世代に)伝える
- **passage** 名 ①通過, 通行, 通路 ②一節, 経過
- **passageway** 名 通路, 廊下
- **passing** 形 通り過ぎる, 一時的な
- **passion** 名 情熱, (～への)熱中, 激怒
- **passionate** 形 情熱的な, (感情が)激しい, 短気な
- **passive** 形 ①消極的な, やる気のない ②(文法の)受動態の, 受け身の
- **past** 形 過去の, この前の 前《時間・場所》を過ぎて, ～を越して 副 通り越して, 過ぎて **walk past** 通り過ぎる
- **paste** 動 のりで貼る
- **path** 名 ①(踏まれてできた)小道, 歩道 ②進路, 通路
- **pathetic** 形 哀れな, 感傷的な
- **patient** 名 病人, 患者
- **patiently** 副 我慢強く, 根気よく
- **pattern** 名 柄, 型, 模様
- **pause** 動 休止する, 立ち止まる
- **pay** 動 ①支払う, 払う, 報いる, 償う ②割に合う, ペイする **pay attention** 注意［留意・注目］する
- **peacefully** 副 平和に, 穏やかに
- **peak** 名 頂点, 最高点
- **peal** 名 (鐘の)響き, (雷, 笑いの)とどろき
- **peer** 動 じっと見る
- **per** 前 ～につき, ～ごとに **as per** ～のとおり
- **perceive** 動 ～を理解する, ～だとわかる
- **percentage** 名 パーセンテージ, 割合, 比率
- **perfectly** 副 完全に, 申し分なく
- **perhaps** 副 たぶん, ことによると
- **permanent** 形 永続する, 永久の, 長持ちする
- **permit** 動 ①許可する ②(物・事が)可能にする
- **persist** 動 ①固執する, 主張する ②続く, 存続する
- **personal** 形 ①個人の, 私的な ②本人自らの
- **perspective** 名 観点
- **peruse** 動 熟読する
- **perverse** 形 ひねくれた
- **perversity** 名 つむじ曲がり, 強情
- **photograph** 名 写真
- **phrase** 名 句, 慣用句, 名言
- **physical** 形 ①物質の, 物理学の, 自然科学の ②身体の, 肉体の
- **physician** 名 医師, 医者
- **physique** 名 体格, 体形
- **pile** 動 積み重ねる, 積もる
- **pinch** 動 つまむ, はさむ
- **pitch** 名 ピッチ《原油・石油タール・木タールなどを蒸留した後に残る黒色のかす》 **pick black** 漆黒 **pick dark** 真っ暗
- **pitiable** 形 哀れな, 惨めな
- **pitiably** 哀れなことに
- **pitiful** 形 ①哀れな, 痛々しい ②浅ましい
- **place** 熟 **take place** 行われる, 起こる
- **placement** 名 配置, 配列
- **plain** 形 ①明白な, はっきりした ②簡素な
- **platform** 名 プラットホーム, 壇
- **play a part** 役目を果たす
- **play with** ～で遊ぶ, ～と一緒に遊ぶ
- **please** 動 満足させる, 喜ばせる

Word List

- **pleasure** 名 喜び, 楽しみ, 満足, 娯楽
- **plenty** 名 十分, たくさん, 豊富 plenty of たくさんの〜
- **plop** 動 ドサッと落ちる[落とす] plop down ドスンと座る
- **plot** 名 構想, 筋立て, プロット, 策略
- **plow** 動 すく, 耕す plow ahead 進行していく
- **plum** 名 セイヨウスモモ, プラム
- **plump** 形 太り気味の, ふっくらした, ぽっちゃりした
- **plunk** 動 (重いものを)ドスンと落とす
- **ply** 動 (道具などを)せっせと使う
- **Poe** 名 (エドガー・アラン・)ポー《アメリカの小説家, 詩人》
- **poet** 名 詩人, 歌人
- **point** 熟 at this point 現在のところ to the point 要領を得た
- **police force** 警官隊
- **policeman** 名 警察官
- **political** 形 ①政治の, 政党の ②策略的な
- **politician** 名 政治家, 政略家
- **ponderously** 副 重々しく
- **pop** 動 ポンと鳴る
- **porch** 名 ポーチ, 玄関, 車寄せ
- **portion** 名 一部, 分け前
- **position** 名 位置, 場所, 姿勢
- **possess** 動 ①持つ, 所有する ②(心などを)保つ, 制御する
- **possessor** 名 所有者
- **possible** 形 ①可能な ②ありうる, 起こりうる if possible できるなら
- **possibly** 副 ①あるいは, たぶん ②《否定文, 疑問文で》どうしても, できる限り, とても, なんとか
- **pot** 名 壺, (深い)なべ
- **pour** 動 ①注ぐ, 浴びせる ②流れ出る, 流れ込む ③ざあざあ降る
- **powder** 名 粉末
- **powerful** 形 強い, 実力のある, 影響力のある
- **practical** 形 ①実際的な, 実用的な, 役に立つ ②経験を積んだ
- **prayer** 名 ①祈り, 祈願(文) ②祈る人
- **precisely** 副 正確に, ちょうど
- **preeminently** 副 卓越して, 著しく
- **preference** 名 好きであること, 好み
- **preliminary** 形 予備の, 前置きの
- **premonition** 名 予感, 兆候
- **presence** 名 ①存在すること ②出席, 態度
- **president** 名 ①大統領 ②社長, 学長, 頭取
- **press** 動 ①圧する, 押す, プレスする ②強要する, 迫る
- **pressure** 名 プレッシャー, 圧力, 圧縮, 重荷
- **presumptuous** 形 出しゃばった, おこがましい
- **previous** 形 前の, 先の
- **previously** 副 あらかじめ, 以前に[は]
- **pride** 名 誇り, 自慢, 自尊心
- **primarily** 副 第一に, 最初に, 根本的に
- **probably** 副 たぶん, あるいは
- **probe** 動 徹底的に調査する, 探りを入れる
- **probing** 形 厳密な, 徹底した
- **proceed** 動 進む, 進展する, 続ける
- **process** 名 ①過程, 経過, 進行 ②手順, 方法, 製法, 加工
- **profession** 名 職業, 専門職
- **professional** 形 専門の, プロの,

職業的な
- **profitable** 形 利益になる, 有益な
- **progress** 名 ①進歩, 前進 ②成り行き, 経過
- **project** 名 計画, プロジェクト
- **prolix** 形 長ったらしい, 冗長な
- **proof** 名 証拠, 証明
- **proportion** 名 ①割合, 比率, 分け前 ②釣り合い, 比例
- **proprietor** 名 持ち主, 所有者
- **propriety** 名 ①妥当, 適正 ②礼儀正しさ, 《the -ties》作法
- **prosaic** 形 散文の, 平凡な
- **prosecutor** 名 ①検察官 ②訴追者
- **prostrate** 動 ひざまずかせる, ひれ伏させる
- **protuberance** 名 突起(物)
- **prove** 動 ①証明する ②(〜であることが) わかる, (〜と) なる
- **provide** 動 ①供給する, 用意する, (〜に) 備える ②規定する
- **provoke** 動 ①怒らせる ②刺激して〜させる ③引き起こす
- **prowl** 動 うろつく
- **pry** 動 詮索する, 首を突っ込む
- **psychological** 形 心理学の, 精神の, 心理的な
- **psychologically** 副 心理的に, 心理学的に
- **psychologist** 名 心理学者, 精神分析医
- **psychology** 名 心理学, 心理, 性格
- **public** 形 公の, 公開の
- **publish** 動 ①発表[公表]する ②出版[発行]する
- **pull off** 離れる, 去る, (衣服などを) 脱ぐ
- **pull out** 引き抜く, 引き出す, 取り出す
- **pull up** 引っ張り上げる
- **punishment** 名 ①罰, 処罰 ②罰を受けること
- **purchase** 動 購入する, 獲得する
- **purchaser** 名 購入者, 買い手
- **pure** 形 ①純粋な, 混じりけのない ②罪のない, 清い
- **purple** 形 紫色の
- **purse** 名 ①財布, 小銭入れ ②小物入れ
- **put oneself in someone's shoes** (人の) 立場になって考える
- **put up** 〜を上げる, 揚げる, 建てる, 飾る
- **put ~ into ...** 〜を…に入れ込む
- **putrid** 形 腐敗した, 悪臭を放つ

Q

- **quality** 名 ①質, 性質, 品質 ②特性 ③良質
- **question** 熟 in question 問題の, 論争中の
- **quickly** 副 敏速に, 急いで
- **quietly** 副 ①静かに ②平穏に, 控えめに

R

- **rainbow** 名 虹
- **raise** 動 ①上げる, 高める ②起こす ③〜を育てる
- **range** 名 列, 連なり, 範囲
- **rank** 名 ①列 ②階級, 位
- **rapidly** 副 速く, 急速, すばやく, 迅速に
- **rare** 形 まれな, 珍しい
- **rarely** 副 めったに〜しない, まれに, 珍しいほど

Word List

- **rate** 图 ①割合, 率 ②相場, 料金 **at any rate** とにかく, 何しろ
- **rather** 副 ①むしろ, かえって ②かなり, いくぶん, やや ③それどころか逆に **rather than** ~よりむしろ
- **rattling** 形 ガラガラいう[音を立てる]
- **reaction** 图 反応, 反動, 反抗, 影響
- **read through** ~を読み通す
- **reader** 图 読者
- **reality** 图 現実, 実在, 真実(性)
- **realize** 動 理解する, 実現する
- **reason** 熟 **for some reason** なんらかの理由で, どういうわけか **reason for** ~の理由
- **reasoning** 图 推理, 推論, 論拠
- **rebuilt** 動 rebuild(再建する)の過去, 過去分詞
- **recent** 形 近ごろの, 近代の
- **recently** 副 近ごろ, 最近
- **reconfigure** 图 再構成する
- **reconnect** 動 再びつながる, 再接続される
- **record** 图 記録, 登録, 履歴
- **recount** 動 ①詳しく話す ②数え直す, 列挙する
- **recover** 動 ①取り戻す, ばん回する ②回復する
- **rectangular** 形 長方形の, 直角の
- **reduce** 動 ①減じる ②しいて~させる, (~の)状態にする
- **refer** 動 ①《- to ~》~に言及する, ~と呼ぶ, ~を指す ②~を参照する, ~に問い合わせる
- **reference** 图 言及, 参照, 照会
- **refrain** 動 差し控える, 自制する **refrain from** ~を控える, ~を遠慮する
- **regard** 動 ①《~を…と》見なす ②尊敬する, 重きを置く ③関係がある
- **regarding** 前 ~に関しては, ~について
- **regardless** 副 それにもかかわらず, それでも
- **regrettably** 副 残念ながら
- **regular** 形 ①規則的な, 秩序のある ②定期的な, 一定の, 習慣的
- **rehearse** 動 リハーサル[下稽古]をする, ~を習熟させる
- **rejoin** 動 復帰する, 再び一緒になる
- **relation** 图 ①(利害)関係, 間柄 ②親戚
- **relationship** 图 関係, 関連, 血縁関係
- **relative** 形 関係のある, 相対的な
- **relatively** 副 比較的, 相対的に
- **relevance** 图 関連(性), つながり
- **relief** 图 (苦痛・心配などの)除去, 軽減, 安心, 気晴らし
- **rely** 動 (人が…に)頼る, 当てにする
- **remain** 動 ①残っている, 残る ②(~の)ままである[いる]
- **remind** 動 思い出させる, 気づかせる
- **renewal** 图 更新, 書き換え, 再開発
- **rent** 動 賃借りする
- **repeat** 動 繰り返す
- **repel** 動 (攻撃や侵略を)撃退する
- **reply** 動 答える, 返事をする, 応答する 图 答え, 返事, 応答
- **reporter** 图 レポーター, 報告者, 記者
- **repose** 動 休ませる, 休む, 横たわる
- **reproduce** 動 ①再生する, 再現する ②複写する, 模造する
- **repudiate** 動 否認する, 拒絶する
- **repulsive** 形 ひどく不快な, 忌まわしい

- □ **reputation** 名 評判, 名声, 世評
- □ **repute** 名 評判, 世評
- □ **request** 名 願い, 要求(物), 需要 動 求める, 申し込む
- □ **require** 動 ①必要とする, 要する ②命じる, 請求する
- □ **resemblance** 名 類似(点), 似ていること
- □ **residence** 名 住宅, 居住
- □ **resident** 名 居住者, 在住者
- □ **residue** 名 残り, 残余
- □ **resist** 動 抵抗[反抗・反撃]する, 耐える
- □ **resolve** 動 決心する, 解決する
- □ **respect** 名 ①尊敬, 尊重 ②注意, 考慮
- □ **respectable** 形 ①尊敬すべき, 立派な ②(量など)相当な
- □ **respond** 動 答える, 返答[応答]する
- □ **response** 名 応答, 反応, 返答
- □ **result** 名 結果, 成り行き, 成績 **as a result** その結果(として) **as a result of** ～の結果(として)
- □ **resuscitate** 動 蘇生させる
- □ **resuscitation** 名 蘇生させる
- □ **retreat** 動 後退する, 退く
- □ **return to** ～に戻る, ～に帰る
- □ **reveal** 動 明らかにする, 暴露する, もらす
- □ **reverence** 名 尊敬, 崇拝
- □ **revolver** 名 回転式拳銃, リボルバー
- □ **reward** 動 報いる, 報酬を与える
- □ **richly** 副 ぜいたくに, 豪華に, 十分に
- □ **rip** 動 引き裂く, 切り裂く, 破る **rip up** ビリビリに裂く
- □ **rise to one's feet** 立ち上がる
- □ **risk** 名 危険
- □ **risky** 形 危険な, 冒険的な, リスクの伴う
- □ **robber** 名 泥棒, 強盗
- □ **robbery** 名 泥棒, 強盗
- □ **romantic** 形 ロマンチックな, 空想的な
- □ **roof** 名 屋根, 屋上
- □ **Rose Delacourt case** ローズ・デラクール事件《『モルグ街の殺人』のモデルとなった事件》
- □ **rote** 名 決まりきったやり方, 機械的手順
- □ **rough** 形 ①(手触りが)粗い ②荒々しい, 未加工の
- □ **roughly** 副 ①おおよそ, 概略的に, 大ざっぱに ②手荒く, 粗雑に
- □ **round** 熟 **make a round of** あちこちの～を訪れる
- □ **route** 名 道, 道筋, 進路, 回路
- □ **routine** 名 お決まりの手順, 日課
- □ **row** 名 (横に並んだ)列 **row house** 長屋
- □ **rubber** 名 ゴム, 消しゴム
- □ **rubbernecker** 名 やじ馬
- □ **rude** 形 粗野な, 無作法な, 失礼な
- □ **rudely** 副 無礼に, 手荒く
- □ **rudeness** 名 無礼, 不作法
- □ **Rue Morgue, The Murder in the** 『モルグ街の殺人』《エドガー・アラン・ポーによる短編推理小説》
- □ **ruffle** 動 (鳥の羽などが)逆立つ
- □ **ruin** 動 破滅させる
- □ **rumor** 名 うわさ
- □ **rumpus** 名 大騒ぎ, 騒動
- □ **run about** 走り回る
- □ **run off** 走り去る, 逃げ去る
- □ **run one's eyes over** ～にザッと目を通す
- □ **run over** 一走りする, ～の上を走る, ひき[押し]倒す

Word List

- **run through** 走り抜ける
- **running** 熟 come running 飛んでくる, かけつける
- **rush** 動 突進する, せき立てる rush in ～に突入する, ～に駆けつける
- **rustle** 名 さらさらという音

S

- **sacred** 形 神聖な, 厳粛な
- **sadist** 名 サディスト, 加虐性愛者
- **same ~ as ...** 《the –》…と同じ(ような)～
- **sample** 名 見本, 標本
- **sank** 動 sink(沈む)の過去
- **sash** 名 サッシ, 窓枠
- **satisfaction** 名 満足
- **satisfy** 動 ①満足させる, 納得させる ②(義務を)果たす, 償う
- **scent** 名 (快い)におい, 香り
- **scholar** 名 学者
- **scholarly** 副 学問的な, 学者らしい
- **scientific** 形 科学の, 科学的な
- **scoot** 動 急いで行く scoot back to ～へ逃げ帰る
- **scrap** 名 切れ端, くず, スクラップ
- **screen** 名 仕切り, 幕, スクリーン, 画面 sliding screen 障子
- **scrunch** 動 うずくまる scrunch up 縮こまる
- **scuffle** 名 取っ組み合い, もみ合い, 小競り合い
- **sculpture** 名 ①彫刻 ②彫刻作品
- **scuttle** 動 急いで行く, ちょこちょこ走る
- **seal** 名 印, 封印
- **search** 動 捜し求める, 調べる 名 捜査, 探索, 調査

- **seat** 熟 take a back seat 二の次になる take a seat 席にすわる
- **second-hand** 形 中古の, 古物の
- **second-story** 形 2階の
- **secondhand** 形 中古の secondhand bookstore 古書店
- **secret** 形 秘密の, 隠れた
- **secretary** 名 秘書, 書記
- **secretly** 副 秘密に, 内緒で
- **see** 熟 Let me see. ええと。 see off 見送る you see あのね, いいですか
- **seem** 動 (～に)見える, (～のように)思われる seem to be ～であるように思われる
- **seemingly** 副 見たところでは, 外見は
- **self** 名 ①自己, ～そのもの ②私利, 私欲, 利己主義 ③自我
- **seller** 名 売る人, 売れるもの
- **send for** ～を呼びにやる, ～を呼び寄せる
- **sensation** 名 ①感覚, 感じ ②大評判, センセーション
- **sense** 名 ①感覚, 感じ ②《-s》意識, 正気, 本性 ③常識, 分別, センス ④意味 動 感じる, 気づく
- **sensibility** 名 感覚, 識別能力, 《-ties》感受性
- **sensible** 形 ①分別のある ②理にかなっている ③気づいている
- **sensibly** 副 (言動などが)分別よく
- **sensual** 形 官能的な, 肉感的な
- **sentimental** 形 感傷的な, 情にもろい, 涙もろい, 感情的な
- **separate** 動 ①分ける, 分かれる, 隔てる ②別れる, 別れさせる 形 分かれれた, 別れた, 別々の under separate cover 別封で
- **series** 名 一続き, 連続, シリーズ
- **serious** 形 ①まじめな, 真剣な ②

重大な, 深刻な, (病気などが)重い

- **servant** 名 ①召使, 使用人, しもべ ②公務員, (公共事業の)従業員 civil servant 公務員
- **set out** ①出発する, 置く ②配置する
- **set to** 《be –》~することになって[決まって]いる
- **settle** 動 ①安定する[させる], 落ち着く, 落ち着かせる ②《- in ~》~に移り住む, 定住する settle down 落ち着く, 興奮がおさまる
- **sex** 名 性, 性別, 男女
- **shabby** 形 みすぼらしい, 粗末な, 貧相な, 卑しい
- **Shabby-looking** 形 ぼろぼろの, みすぼらしい
- **shadow** 名 ①影, 暗がり ②亡霊
- **shake** 動 振る, 揺れる, 揺さぶる, 震える
- **shakuhachi** 名 尺八
- **Shall we ~?** (一緒に)~しましょうか。
- **shame** 名 ①恥, 恥辱 ②恥ずべきこと, ひどいこと
- **shameless** 形 恥知らずの
- **shape** 名 ①形, 姿, 型
- **sharp** 形 鋭い, とがった
- **sheer** 形 ①まったくの, 純粋の ②切り立った
- **sheet** 名 ①シーツ ②(紙などの)1枚
- **shelf** 名 棚
- **shell** 名 ①貝がら, (木の実・卵などの)から ②(建物の)骨組み
- **shift** 動 移す, 変える
- **shoji** 名 障子
- **shoplifter** 名 万引き犯人
- **short** 熟 in short 要約すると
- **shortly** 副 まもなく, すぐに
- **shot** 熟 give it a shot 一丁やってみる
- **should have done** ~すべきだった(のにしなかった)《仮定法》
- **shoulder** 名 肩 shoulder blade 肩甲骨
- **shove** 動 乱暴に押す, 押し込む, 突く when push comes shove いざとなると
- **shrewdly** 副 鋭く
- **shrivel** 形 しなびた
- **shudder** 動 身震いする, 震える
- **shut** 動 ①閉まる, 閉める, 閉じる ②たたむ ③閉じ込める ④shutの過去, 過去分詞
- **sickly** 形 病弱な, 青ざめた, 健康に悪い, うんざりする
- **sickness** 名 病気
- **side** 名 側, 横, そば, 斜面 either side of ~の両側に on either side 両側に one side 片側
- **sigh** 動 ため息をつく, ため息をついて言う
- **signal** 名 信号, 合図
- **silent** 形 ①無言の, 黙っている ②静かな, 音を立てない ③活動しない
- **silently** 副 静かに, 黙って
- **similar** 形 同じような, 類似した, 相似の
- **simple-look** 形 一見[表面的には]簡単に見える
- **simply** 副 ①簡単に ②単に, ただ ③まったく, 完全に
- **since** 熟 ever since それ以来ずっと
- **sincerely** 副 真心をこめて
- **single** 形 ①たった1つの ②1人用の, それぞれの 動 ~を選び出す single out (複数の候補[者]から)~を選び出す
- **sip** 動 (酒・茶などを)少しずつ飲む, ちびちび飲む
- **sit on** ~の上に乗る, ~の上に乗っ

WORD LIST

て動けないようにする
- □ **situate** 動 (ある場所に)置く, 位置づける
- □ **situation** 名 ①場所, 位置 ②状況, 境遇, 立場
- □ **six-mat room** 六畳間
- □ **skeleton** 名 骨格, がい骨, 骨組み
- □ **skillful** 形 熟練した, 腕のいい
- □ **sleep in** 寝床に入る, 朝寝坊する, 住み込む
- □ **sleeve** 名 袖, たもと, スリーブ
- □ **slender** 形 ①ほっそりとした ②わずかな
- □ **slid** 動 slide (滑る) の過去, 過去分詞
- □ **sliding** 形 滑る, スライドする sliding screen 障子
- □ **slight** 形 ①わずかな ②ほっそりして ③とるに足らない
- □ **slightly** 副 わずかに, いささか
- □ **slip** 動 滑る, 滑らせる, 滑って転ぶ slip out of ～からそっと抜け出す [ひそかに離れる]
- □ **slit** 名 (細長い)切り込み, 開口部
- □ **slowly** 副 遅く, ゆっくり
- □ **smoke** 動 喫煙する, 煙を出す 名 煙, 煙状のもの
- □ **snake** 名 ヘビ(蛇)
- □ **sneak** 動 ①こそこそする ②こっそり持ち出す, くすねる sneak into ～に忍び込む
- □ **so** 熟 and so そこで, それだから, それで and so on ～など, その他もろもろ not so ～ as … …ほど～でない not so much as ～ほどではない so ～ as to … …するほど~できるように so ～ that … 非常に~なので…
- □ **soba** 名 そば
- □ **social** 形 ①社会の, 社会的な ②社交的な, 愛想のよい
- □ **soft-look** 形 柔らかそうに見える
- □ **softly** 副 柔らかに, 優しく, そっと
- □ **solid** 形 色が同一の, 濃淡のない, ベタの solid white 白一色の
- □ **solution** 名 解決, 解明, 回答
- □ **solve** 動 解く, 解決する
- □ **some** 熟 for some reason なんらかの理由で, どういうわけか for some time しばらくの間 some time いつか, そのうち
- □ **somehow** 副 ①どうにかこうにか, ともかく, 何とかして ②どういうわけか
- □ **someone** 代 ある人, 誰か
- □ **something** 代 ①ある物, 何か ②いくぶん, 多少
- □ **Something Mile Road** 何問道路とかいう大通り
- □ **sometimes** 副 時々, 時たま
- □ **somewhat** 副 いくらか, やや, 多少
- □ **somewhere** 副 ①どこかへ[に] ②いつか, およそ
- □ **soon** 熟 as soon as ～するとすぐ, ～するや否や
- □ **sooner** 熟 no sooner ～するや否や
- □ **sordid** 形 ①卑劣な, 浅ましい ②汚い, むさ苦しい ③くすんだ色の
- □ **sort** 名 種類, 品質 a sort of ～のようなもの, 一種の～ no sort of いかなる～も全くない what sort of どういう
- □ **soul** 名 ①魂 ②精神, 心
- □ **source** 名 源, 原因, もと
- □ **speak of** ～を口にする
- □ **specialist** 名 専門家, スペシャリスト
- □ **specialty** 名 専門, 専攻, 本職, 得意
- □ **species** 名 種, 種類, 人種

- **specific** 形 明確な, はっきりした, 具体的な
- **speckled** 形 たくさんの小さな斑点のついた Adventure of the Speckled Band『まだらの紐』《アーサー・コナン・ドイルによる短編小説》
- **speed** 名 速力, 速度
- **spider** 名 クモ(蜘蛛)
- **spill** 動 こぼす, まき散らす
- **spine** 名 背骨, 脊柱
- **spirit** 名 ①霊 ②精神, 気力
- **spitting image** 生き写し, うり二つ
- **spite** 名 悪意, うらみ in spite of ~にもかかわらず
- **splash** 動 (水・泥を)はね飛ばす
- **splendid** 形 見事な, 壮麗な, 堂々とした
- **split** 動 裂く, 裂ける, 割る, 割れる, 分裂させる[する] split up (集団が)分かれる
- **spontaneously** 副 自発的に, 無意識のうちに, 自然に
- **spot** 名 ①地点, 場所, 立場 ②斑点, しみ blind spot (見落しがちな)盲点
- **spouse** 名 配偶者
- **sprang** 動 spring (跳ねる)の過去
- **spring to one's feet** 飛び上がる
- **springy** 形 弾力(性)のある
- **sprinkle** 動 振りかける, 散布する
- **spur** 動 拍車をかける, 駆り立てる
- **squalid** 形 むさ苦しい, 卑しい
- **square** 形 ①正方形の, 四角な, 直角な, 角ばった ②平方の square feet 平方フィート
- **square-printed paper** (マス目の入った)原稿用紙
- **squeeze** 動 絞る, 強く握る, 締めつける
- **stack** 名 ①大きな山, 積み重ね ②多量, 多数 動 積み重ねる
- **stair** 名 ①(階段の)1段 ②《-s》階段, はしご
- **staircase** 名 階段
- **stamp** 動 踏みつける
- **stand by** そばに立つ, 傍観する, 待機する
- **stand out** 突き出る, 目立つ
- **stare** 動 じっと[じろじろ]見る
- **start** 熟 give a start びくっとする
- **startling** 形 びっくりさせる, 仰天させる
- **state** 名 あり様, 状態 動 述べる, 表明する
- **statement** 名 声明, 述べること
- **status** 名 ①(社会的な)地位, 身分, 立場 ②状態
- **stay in** 家にいる, (場所に)泊まる, 滞在する
- **steal** 動 盗む
- **stealing** 名 窃盗
- **steel** 動 (人)を非情にする steel oneself 覚悟を決める
- **stick** 動 ①(突き)刺さる, 刺す ②くっつく, くっつける ③突き出る ④《受け身形で》いきづまる stick out of ~から突き出す
- **stock** 動 蓄える
- **stolen** 動 steal (盗む)の過去分詞
- **stolid** 形 ぼんやりした
- **storage** 名 ①貯蔵, 倉庫
- **storefront** 名 店の正面, 店頭
- **storeroom** 名 保管室, 物置
- **storyteller** 名 物語をする人, 物語作家
- **strain** 動 ①緊張させる, ぴんと張る ②無理に曲げる
- **strangely** 副 奇妙に, 変に, 不思議なことに, 不慣れに

Word List

- **stranger** 名 ①見知らぬ人, 他人 ②不案内[不慣れ]な人
- **strangle** 動 窒息死させる, 絞め殺す
- **strangulation** 名 絞殺
- **strength** 名 ①力, 体力 ②長所, 強み ③強度, 濃度
- **stretch** 動 引き伸ばす, 広がる, 広げる
- **strike** 動 ①打つ, ぶつかる ②(災害などが)急に襲う
- **strip** 名 (細長い)1片
- **stripe** 名 筋, 縞, ストライプ block stripe 棒縞
- **striped** 形 筋の入った, 縞模様の
- **stroll** 動 ぶらぶら歩く, 散歩する
- **strong-headed** 形 頑固な, 強情な
- **struck** 動 strike (打つ)の過去, 過去分詞
- **struggle** 動 もがく, 奮闘する 名 もがき, 奮闘
- **strut** 動 もったいぶって歩く strut about のさばり歩く
- **stuck** 動 stick (刺さる)の過去, 過去分詞 be stuck いきづまる
- **stumble** 動 ①よろめく, つまずく ②偶然出会う
- **stupefy** 動 ぼうぜんとさせる
- **stupor** 名 意識もうろう, 放心状態
- **sturdy** 形 屈強な, 頑丈な
- **success** 名 成功, 幸運, 上首尾
- **successful** 形 成功した, うまくいった
- **such a** そのような
- **such as** たとえば〜, 〜のような such 〜 as … …のような〜
- **such 〜 that …** 非常に〜なので…
- **sufficiently** 副 十分に, 足りて
- **suggest** 動 ①提案する ②示唆する
- **suit** 名 スーツ, 背広
- **sultry** 形 蒸し暑い
- **sum** 名 ①総計 ②金額
- **sumptuous** 形 豪華な, ぜいたくな
- **sunset** 名 日没, 夕焼け
- **sunshine** 名 日光
- **superficial** 形 表面の, うわべだけの
- **superiority** 名 優勢, 優越, 優位(性)
- **supple** 形 ①柔軟な, よく曲がる ②素直な, 従順な
- **support** 動 支える, 支持する
- **suppose** 動 仮定する, 推測する
- **supremely** 副 最高に, 極めて
- **sure** 熟 be sure to do 必ず〜する for sure 確かに sure enough 思ったとおり, 確かに
- **surely** 副 確かに, きっと
- **surpass** 動 勝る, しのぐ
- **surprise** 熟 taken by surprise 不意を付かれる, 寝耳に水である to one's surprise 〜が驚いたことに
- **surprised** 形 驚いた
- **surprising** 形 驚くべき, 意外な
- **surround** 動 囲む, 包囲する
- **susceptible** 形 ①影響を受けやすい ②多感な, 敏感な ③受け入れる余地がある
- **suspect** 動 疑う, (〜ではないかと)思う 名 容疑者, 注意人物
- **suspected** 形 疑わしい
- **suspicion** 名 ①容疑, 疑い ②感づくこと
- **suspicious** 形 あやしい, 疑い深い
- **swagger** 動 いばって歩く swagger around ふんぞり返って歩き回る

143

- □ **sweat** 名 汗
- □ **sweetness** 名 ①甘さ ②優しさ, 美しさ
- □ **swiftly** 副 速く, 迅速に
- □ **swing** 動 揺り動かす, 揺れる
- □ **switch** 名 スイッチ 動 ①スイッチを入れる[切る] ②切り替える, 切り替わる
- □ **swore** 動 swear（誓う）の過去
- □ **sworn** 動 swear（誓う）の過去分詞
- □ **synthesis** 名 総合, 合成, 統合体

T

- □ **tabi** 名 足袋
- □ **tail** 名 ①尾, しっぽ ②後部, 末尾 tail bone 尾骨
- □ **taint** 動 汚れる, 感染する
- □ **Taisho Era** 大正時代
- □ **take** 熟 take a back seat 二の次になる take a look at ～をちょっと見る take a seat 席にすわる take away ①連れ去る ②取り上げる, 奪い去る ③取り除く take care 気をつける, 注意する take down 引き下げる, 降ろす take in 取り入れる, 取り込む, (作物・金などを)集める take long 時間がかかる take place 行われる, 起こる take someone through (人)に(場所)を通らせる take ～ to … ～を…に連れて行く take turns to 交代で～する
- □ **taken aback** 驚く, びっくりさせられる, 困惑する
- □ **taken by surprise** 不意をつかれる, 寝耳に水である
- □ **talent** 名 才能, 才能ある人
- □ **tangled** 形 もつれた, 絡みついた
- □ **Tanizaki Jun'ichiro** 谷崎潤一郎《小説家》
- □ **task** 名 (やるべき)仕事, 職務, 課題
- □ **tatami** 名 畳
- □ **technical** 形 技術(上)の, 工業の, 専門の
- □ **technique** 名 テクニック, 技術, 手法
- □ **temporarily** 副 一時的に, 仮に, 当面は
- □ **tenant** 名 賃借人, 住人, テナント
- □ **tend** 動 ①(～の)傾向がある, (～)しがちである ②面倒を見る, 手入れをする
- □ **tender** 形 柔らかい, もろい, 弱い, 優しい
- □ **term** 名 ①期間, 期限 ②語, 用語 ③《-s》条件 ④《-s》関係, 仲 on ～ terms with …… と～な仲である
- □ **terribly** 副 ひどく
- □ **terrifying** 形 恐ろしい
- □ **terror** 名 ①恐怖 ②恐ろしい人[物]
- □ **testimony** 名 証明, 証拠, 証言, 供述
- □ **text** 名 本文, 原本, テキスト, 教科書
- □ **thanks to** ～のおかげで, ～の結果
- □ **that** 熟 now that 今や～だから, ～からには so that ～するために, それで, ～できるように so ～ that … 非常に～なので… such ～ that … 非常に～なので…
- □ **that-a-way** その方向に, あちらへ
- □ **theft** 名 盗み, 窃盗, 泥棒
- □ **then** 熟 by then その時までに just then そのとたんに
- □ **there** 熟 here and there あちこちに over there あそこに there is no way ～する見込みはない
- □ **thereafter** 副 それ以来, 従って
- □ **therefore** 副 したがって, それゆえ, その結果
- □ **thereupon** 副 その後すぐに, その結果
- □ **thick** 形 厚い, 密集した, 濃厚な
- □ **thief** 名 泥棒, 強盗
- □ **thigh** 名 太もも, 大腿部

144

Word List

- **thin** 形 薄い, 細い, やせた, まばらな
- **think** 熟 come to think of it 考えてみると think of ～のことを考える, ～を思いつく, 考え出す
- **this-a-way** こっちに, こちらの方へ
- **thoroughly** 副 すっかり, 徹底的に
- **though** 接 ①～にもかかわらず, ～だが ②たとえ～でも as though あたかも～のように, まるで～みたいに
- **thoughtfully** 副 考え[思いやり]深く
- **thoughtfulness** 名 思慮深さ, 心遣い
- **thrall** 名 奴隷, 奴隷の状態 in thrall とりこになる
- **thrill** 名 スリル, 身震い 動 ぞっとする[させる], わくわくする[させる]
- **throng** 動 群がる, 殺到する be thronged with ～で混雑している
- **throughout** 前 ①～中, ～を通じて ②～のいたるところに
- **throw away** ～を捨てる；～を無駄に費やす, 浪費する
- **thrust** 名 ①ぐいと押すこと, 突き刺すこと ②《the -》要点
- **thumb** 名 親指
- **thumbprint** 名 親指の指紋
- **thump** 名 ①強くなぐること, なぐり合い ②ドシン[ゴツン]という音
- **thunderous** 形 雷のような
- **thus** 副 ①このように ②これだけ ③かくて, だから
- **thusly** 副 示された方法で
- **tightly** 副 きつく, しっかり, 堅く
- **tilt** 動 傾ける, (容器などを)傾けてあける
- **time** 熟 at a time 一度に, 続けざまに at that time その時 by the time ～する時までに every time ～するときはいつも for some time しばらくの間 for the first time in one's life 生まれて初めて for the time being 今のところは in time 調子を合わせて some time いつか, そのうち times as … as A Aの～倍の…
- **tinge** 名 淡い色, 色合い, 気味
- **tiny** 形 ちっぽけな, とても小さい
- **tired** 形 ①疲れた, くたびれた ②あきた, うんざりした
- **title** 名 ①題名, タイトル ②肩書, 称号 ③権利, 資格
- **tobacconist** 名 たばこ屋
- **toil** 動 骨折って働く
- **Tokyo** 名 東京《地名》
- **tomb** 名 墓穴, 墓石, 納骨堂
- **ton** 名 トン《重量・容積単位》
- **tone** 名 音, 音色, 調子
- **too** 熟 far too あまりにも～過ぎる too much 過度の
- **top** 熟 on top of ～の上(部)に
- **topic** 名 話題, 見出し
- **tore** 動 tear(裂く)の過去
- **torment** 動 困らせる, 苦しめる
- **trace** 名 ①跡 ②(事件などの)こん跡
- **track** 名 ①通った跡 ②競走路, 軌道, トラック
- **transform** 動 ①変形[変化]する, 変える ②変換する
- **transmit** 動 ①送る ②伝える, 伝わる ③感染させる
- **transport** 動 輸送[運送]する
- **trap** 名 わな, 策略
- **tread** 名 踏む[歩く]こと, 歩きぶり
- **treatment** 名 ①取り扱い, 待遇 ②治療(法)
- **trembling** 名 震え, 身震い
- **tremendous** 形 すさまじい, とても大きい

- **tremendously** 副恐ろしいほどに, 大いに
- **trick** 名①策略 ②いたずら, 冗談 ③手品, 錯覚 **trick of fate** 運命のいたずら
- **trifling** 形くだらない, ふざけた
- **trigger** 名引き金, きっかけ, 要因 **trigger word** 刺激語
- **trousers** 名ズボン
- **truck** 名トラック, 運搬車
- **truly** 副①全く, 本当に, 真に ②心から, 誠実に
- **trust** 動信用[信頼]する, 委託する
- **trustworthy** 形信用できる, あてになる
- **truth** 名①真理, 事実, 本当 ②誠実, 忠実さ
- **tumble** 動倒れる, 転ぶ, つまずく **tumble down** 崩れ落ちる
- **tungsten** 名タングステン《電球フィラメントなどに使われる》
- **turn** 熟 **take turns to** 交代で~する **turn away** 向こうへ行く, 追い払う, (顔を)そむける, 横を向く **turn down** 曲がって~を行く **turn off** (照明などを)消す **turn on** (スイッチなどを)ひねってつける **turn over** ひっくり返る[返す], 思いめぐらす **turn oneself in** 自首する **turn to** ~の方を向く
- **twist** 動①ねじる, よれる ②~を巻く ③身をよじる 名ねじれ, より合わせること **twist of fate** 運命の意外な展開
- **two** 熟 **a ~ or two** 1~か2~, 2, 3の
- **typical** 形典型的な, 象徴的な

U

- **Ueno** 名上野
- **ugliness** 名醜いこと
- **ugly** 形①醜い, ぶかっこうな ②いやな, 不快な, 険悪な
- **unable** 形《be–to~》~することができない
- **unassuming** 形出しゃばらない, 気取らない, 控えめな
- **unaware** 形無意識の, 気づかない
- **unbelievable** 形信じられない (ほどの), 度のはずれた
- **uncertain** 形不確かな, 確信がない
- **uncomfortable** 形心地よくない
- **uncover** 動ふたを取る, 覆いを取る
- **under way** 進行中で
- **underneath** 前~の下に, ~真下に
- **undershirt** 名アンダーシャツ, 肌着
- **understandable** 形理解できる, わかる
- **understanding** 名理解, 意見の一致, 了解
- **undeserving** 形(称賛・賞罰などに)値しない
- **unduly** 副過度に, 不当に
- **uneasy** 形不安な, 焦って
- **unexpected** 形思いがけない, 予期しない
- **unforeseen** 形予期しない, 不測の
- **unfortunate** 形不運な, あいにくな, 不適切な
- **unfortunately** 副不幸にも, 運悪く
- **unfurl** 動広げる, 展開する
- **unhappy** 形不運な, 不幸な
- **unhealthy** 形健康でない
- **uniformed** 形制服を着た
- **unknowingly** 副知らず知らず, 無意識のうちに